Endpaper photograph: *The Duchess of Roxburghe's silver picnic box*
Page 1: *a duck for Catherine Beloe's farmhouse kitchen*
Frontispiece: *Nicola Cox's kitchen*
Title page: *Kitty Campion's Celebration Salad (see p. 27)*

From a Scottish woman to an Englishwoman with much love.
Christmas 1989

The Englishwoman's Kitchen

The Englishwoman's Kitchen

Edited by Tamasin Day-Lewis
Photographs by Tony Heathcote
Drawings by Tessa Henderson

Chatto & Windus · The Hogarth Press · London

Published in 1983 by
Chatto & Windus · The Hogarth Press
40 William IV Street
London WC2N 4DF

All rights reserved. No part of this
publication may be reproduced, stored in
a retrieval system or transmitted in any
form, or by any means, electronic, mechanical,
photocopying, recording or otherwise, without
the prior permission of the publisher.

BRITISH LIBRARY CATALOGUING IN PUBLICATION DATA

The Englishwoman's kitchen.
  1. Cookery, English
  I. Day-Lewis, Tamasin
641.5942   TX717

ISBN 0 7011 2652 3

Text © Chatto & Windus Ltd 1983
Photographs © Tony Heathcote 1983
Drawings © Tessa Henderson 1983

Designed by Alan Bartram
Phototypeset by Wyvern Typesetting Limited, Bristol
Origination by Waterden Reproduction, London
Printed by William Clowes, Beccles, Suffolk, England

Contents

Preface 7

1   Marika Hanbury Tenison, *Country House Weekends* 9
2   Lady Carey Basset, *A Norfolk Farmhouse Kitchen* 14
3   Catherine Beloe, *A Year in the Life of a Farmhouse Kitchen* 18
4   Kitty Campion, *Herbal Salad Making* 23
5   Mirabel Cecil, *A Feast for Children* 28
6   The Countess of Chichester, *Town and Country Entertaining* 33
7   Lady Silvia Combe, *Grandchildren's Lunch* 38
8   Kate Corbett-Winder, *A Welsh Farmhouse Weekend* 42
9   Nicola Cox, *A Travelling Gourmet* 46
10 Shona Crawford Poole, *Puddings and Pies* 51
11 Tamasin Day-Lewis, *A Game Feast* 57
12 Lady Camilla Dempster, *Infidelity in the Kitchen* 63
13 Lady Margaret Douglas-Home, *A Nostalgic Viennese Evening* 68
14 Rose Elliot, *A Vegetarian Harvest Festival* 71
15 Jane Grigson, *A Summer Lunch* 76
16 Pamela Harlech, *Preserves and Pickles* 82
17 Lady Holborow, *A Feast Fit for Judges* 86
18 The Countess of Lichfield, *A Shooting Picnic* 90
19 Antoinette Lucas, *A Yorkshire Weekend* 94
20 Sarah Lucas, *Cooking for Christmas* 99
21 Lady Lymington, *A London Buffet* 104
22 Cecilia McEwen, *A Hogmanay Breakfast* 109
23 Lady Maclean, *Perfectly Simple Cooking* 112
24 Jane Martin, *A Somerset Weekend* 117
25 The Countess Peel, *A Riverside Barbecue* 122
26 The Duchess of Roxburghe, *A Scottish Grouse Shoot* 126
27 Philippa Scott, *A Mediaeval Feast* 130
28 Fortune Stanley, *Cooking in Cumbria* 136
29 Christina Strutt, *A Summer Picnic* 140
30 Caroline Waldegrave, *A Sophisticated London Dinner* 144

Index 150

Lady Camilla Dempster's home-made pasta

Preface

When Chatto & Windus invited me to edit *The Englishwoman's Kitchen*, I took the opportunity to concentrate as hard on character as on cooking. In fact, that is what differentiates this book from the scores of others that come out every year.

The fun in choosing the thirty contributors was equalled by the satisfaction in concocting the same number of entirely different occasions. However, the portraits that emerged have one thing in common: they share a sense that a kitchen is a very personal place where, at best, those who care about food, be they cooks, food writers or just people preparing delights for their family and friends, find a great deal of pleasure and fulfilment.

The contributors have written with originality, excellence and often great wit, and all of them withstood the lengthy editorial process and the pleas for rewrites with good grace and, I think, better results.

The end product does, I hope, show that the Englishwoman's Kitchen is not just alive but exceptionally well; and that it is a place filled with delicious food cooked very often by extraordinary characters.

I would like to thank Rosalind Bell of Chatto & Windus for all the hard work and good advice she has put into the book, which was her idea. I also owe thanks to Catherine Beloe and Jane Smith for typing the manuscript with supreme precision, and to Robin Hanbury Tenison for kindly allowing us to publish his wife Marika's contribution, written shortly before her death. As a tribute to Marika Hanbury Tenison, her article will appear at the beginning of the book. Otherwise the articles are arranged in alphabetical order according to contributor.

Finally, I would like to thank my husband, John Shearer, for his constantly instructive criticism at all stages from conception to completion, including the challenge of assessing some of the more obscure and problematic dishes.

TAMASIN DAY-LEWIS

Publisher's Note

Imperial and metric measurements are given in these recipes. The metric equivalents vary somewhat as cooks differ in their choice of useful working metric measures, some preferring 30g, for instance, as an approximate equivalent of 1oz, while others prefer 25g.

Where cup measures are used (see pages 37 and 81) the cup measurement is 8fl oz. This is also the American standard cup measurement. It may be useful to mention that the American pint is 16fl oz (whereas the Imperial pint used in Britain is 20fl oz).

Marika Hanbury Tenison

Country House Weekends

When I was young and was asked what I was going to be when I grew up (in that infuriating way grown-ups have of asking those far too young to have any idea), I would answer, 'an eccentric'. It was not the right answer. To be an eccentric was out of the question, I was told crossly by my betters. To be an eccentric one either had to be very rich or very intelligent or *mad*.

It is always fun to prove people wrong. My school said I would never make good at anything. A literary agent and a careers adviser told me in no uncertain way that I should forget all about writing and, finally, in my forties (thirty-five published books later) I have become, on my own ground, a gastronomic eccentric of some repute, operating largely from my thoroughly English kitchen.

I have two different approaches towards budgeting for meals. When cooking normal, everyday meals for the family, I scrimp and save wherever possible, producing good nourishing food at the lowest possible cost, so that when it comes to entertaining I can afford to splash out and give my eccentricities full rein. My joy is in the careful planning and intricacy of producing meals that are fun, frivolous and frankly lavish for friends who come to stay or dine with us at our home in Cornwall. Cooking, I believe, should be fun and a delight; if it is undertaken as a chore and a bore then the food you cook will reflect that mood.

Nothing makes for greater relaxation in one's guests than to get them tucking into delicious food washed down by good wine, and nothing is more fun for the imaginative cook than a challenge. My aim is to make every meal different and I love to vary the ambiance as well as the food.

Take a weekend in the summer, for instance, with sunny weather, around eight guests staying and others coming for lunch and dinner on Saturday and Sunday . . .

Breakfast is an informal flexible meal in the long old-fashioned kitchen decorated like the inside of a gipsy caravan with a long scrubbed pine table, dried flowers and herbs hanging from the red beams and my ancient coal-filled Aga still holding its own in competition with the more sophisticated electric and gas cookers of the 1980s.

Lunch on Saturday, if the weather is good enough, will be a picnic by a nearby lake or a barbecue in the water garden. If the weather is not so good, it will be a farmhouse-style meal in the kitchen again or an impromptu picnic in the library with the furniture pushed back and guests sitting on the floor leaning against brightly coloured cushions. There is always a first course even on the most simple of outdoor excursions since this is my favourite form of food. I pay a lot of attention to the form and colour of food and almost always include at least one dish of fresh fish caught only the night before on the Cornish coast. Saturday lunch usually includes a substantial tart of some form or another, an invented recipe I'm trying out and which can be made in advance. The first course may be an iced soup garnished with a sorbet of fresh herbs, or a whipped up mixture of sour cream and Boursin, or it will be a sophisticated concoction of fish or shell fish, light but full of flavour and often decorated with marigold petals or shredded lovage leaves from my herb garden.

The main course may consist of a selection of salads, meat, poultry and sometimes fish, and will be served with plenty of crusty fresh bread and Cornish butter. The meal will end with a good selection of cheeses including a real, full-bodied Cheddar, Stilton, and my latest cheese delights, Blue Brie and Explorateur, served (if they are available) with fresh peaches or nectarines from my greenhouse – if you have never eaten Brie with a ripe peach try it immediately!

But it is in the evening that I really like to let myself go. When we have guests, we eat dinner in the dining-room at an eleven-foot-long seventeenth-century refectory table with a top made from one piece of rather warped elm which I looked for, and finally found, after a fifteen-year search.

I like to have at least five courses in the evening, but prefer six, with the emphasis on the savoury rather than the sweet dish. There is usually a soup to start, with a savoury toast served on the side. Then there will be a light hot or cold dish of eggs, fish or even just vegetables. The main course will usually be based on meat or poultry and I will carve and serve it in the kitchen, accompanying it with as many young and crisply cooked vegetables as I can lay my hands on. Then there might be an ice cream served with a sauce and accompanied by sweet biscuits, followed by a savoury, if possible a newcomer to my repertoire. Finally I will bring on a cheese board and slices of fresh fruit peeled, cored, and arranged on a large circular plate on a bed of crushed ice.

On Sunday I am usually up at the crack of dawn planning something 'special' for Sunday lunch. One Sunday during the early summer is devoted to 'The Bluebell Picnic', a gloriously Edwardian affair sited at the bottom of an ancient slope of thickly carpeted bluebells which runs down to a stream and is shaded by elderly statesmen beech trees. Guests are asked to wear Edwardian clothes and eat on rugs laid under the trees, choosing their food from tables covered with starched white damask cloths and laid with silver. There will probably be about twelve or more dishes to choose from, with a first, main and pudding course, fruit and cheese; Bloody Marys to start with and perhaps a huge raised game pie as a centrepiece. It is a lot of work to plan and prepare but the gratification I get from my guests' enjoyment is worth every moment of the effort. Cookery, for me, is my way of expressing my love and fondness for my family and friends, and their appreciation of my efforts is my reward.

On other Sundays in the summer I serve lunch outside in our walled patio under a cloister garlanded with passion flowers, surrounded by brilliant geraniums and potted plants. This is my 'joke' time when I produce a meal in which every course includes strawberries (iced strawberry soup; marinated fish salad with strawberries, poached poussin with fennel and sliced strawberries, and strawberry and ginger pudding with whipped cream and Cornish Fairings); a lavish Chinese banquet cooked in front of guests in a wok on a strong calor-gas burner; an all-Italian meal with home-made pasta to start with, coloured almost every hue of the rainbow, from beetroot juice, spinach, saffron, tomato and borage. A portable barbecue is often brought into use for these occasions, and the meals usually last for hours.

I am lucky because I almost always have help in my kitchen, and although those that help me must often think I am mad as I clutch my forehead and go into ecstasies about some new dish I have thought up, they are remarkably patient with my eccentricities. I am also lucky because I have the most wonderful gardener who, like Mr MacGregor, keeps me well in order and gives me hearty tickings off for pinching the vegetables before he feels they have matured properly. He provides me with a choice of fresh vegetables including some exotic strains like miniature tomatoes, white aubergines, golden beetroot and golden courgettes. We grow mangetout peas too, and French beans no thicker than a knitting needle, and our herb garden, despite being 850 feet above sea level, is a convenient joy outside the back door.

Although I have to spend some of my time in London, where I have a small mews house, my real joy is cooking in my Cornish kitchen, with the farm just outside the door, the garden stretching down the hill and the comfort of well-used and well-tried equipment. Add to this a handful of favourite guests who leave the house comfortably replete and happier than when they arrived, and you have the ingredients for my favourite recipe. I can think of no other that gives me greater pleasure.

Consommé Madrilène suprême (serves 6)

2 tins consommé
450ml (¾pt) tomato juice
4 firm ripe tomatoes
salt and freshly ground black pepper
a few drops Tabasco sauce
pinch oregano
juice of 1 lemon
4 tablespoons vodka
small jar red caviar (salmon roe)
1 carton (150g) sour cream
1 teaspoon finely chopped parsley
1 small hard-boiled egg, finely chopped

Cover the tomatoes with boiling water for 2 minutes, drain, remove the skins, discard the cores and seeds, and finely chop the flesh. Heat 150ml (¼pt) of the consommé until melted and mix in the tomato juice, vodka, lemon juice, oregano and Tabasco, season with salt, and mix in the rest of the consommé and chopped tomato. Chill in the refrigerator until semi-jelled and ice-cold. Whip the soup with a fork and divide between six bowls. Top each serving with a dollop of sour cream, a spoonful of caviar, and a little finely chopped parsley and hard-boiled egg. Serve well chilled with brown toast.

Sorbet of fresh herbs (serves 6)

A wonderfully refreshing garnish for cold soups (add a couple of teaspoons at the last minute before serving) that can also be used (double the quantities) as a starter by filling three small hollowed-out tomatoes with the sorbet.

175ml (7fl oz) water
1 handful fresh basil leaves
pinch of thyme and sage
juice ½ lemon
3 crisp eating apples (Cox or Granny Smith)
2 egg whites

Bring the water and lemon juice to the boil, throw in the herbs and blanch them for 1 minute. Remove the herbs with a slotted spoon. Peel, core and roughly chop the apples and add them to the cooking liquid. Bring to the boil and cook over a high heat until the apples are tender and most of the liquid has been absorbed.

Purée the blanched herbs in a liquidiser or food processor. Add the apples and reduce to a smooth purée. Turn the mixture into a plastic container, cook and then freeze until beginning to set around the edges. Whisk the egg whites until stiff. Break up the sorbet and purée the half-frozen mixture in a liquidiser or food processor. Turn into a bowl, fold in the egg whites, and mix lightly. Put into a plastic container and freeze until firm.

Note. If you are using this mixture to fill tomato cases cover the tomatoes with boiling water for two minutes and slide off their skins. Cut 'caps' from the top and carefully scoop out the seeds and core with a teaspoon. Leave upside down to drain, and fill just before serving, with the sorbet mixture. Garnish with mint leaves and serve with hot bread and butter.

Smoked salmon and Arbroath smokie mousse parcels (serves 6)

6 slices (250g/8oz) smoked salmon approx 20cm × 10cm (8 × 4 inches) each
2 Arbroath smokies
180g (6oz) cottage cheese
150ml (¼pt) double cream
1 tablespoon dried grated horseradish or horseradish sauce
2 spring onions finely chopped
salt and freshly ground black pepper
1 dill pickled cucumber, finely chopped
2 tablespoons olive or sunflower oil
fresh dill or fennel
thin slices of lemon to garnish

Skin and bone the smokies and flake the flesh. Beat the cottage cheese until smooth or purée in a liquidiser. Beat the cream until thick. Mix the smokies, horseradish, onion and cucumber into the cheese, season with salt and pepper and lightly fold in the cream. Divide the mousse between the salmon slices, turn in the sides and roll into neat parcels. Chill until five minutes before required.

Brush with a little oil, sprinkle with a little cayenne and heat through (the smoked salmon should be piping hot but the mousse still pleasurably cool) in the bottom of a hot oven (475°F/240°C, gas mark 9) for 5 minutes.

Garnish with sprigs of dill or fennel, and top with one or two slices of lemon.

Beef teriyaki (serves 6)

The success of this dish lies in the very quick cooking which seals and browns the outside, leaving the centre bright pink. Leave the meat to 'settle' for 10 minutes before carving, and cut into wafer-thin slices with a razor-sharp knife.

1.25kg (2½lb) trimmed whole fillet of beef

Marinade
1 tablespoon tomato ketchup
2 tablespoons soy sauce
1 tablespoon soft brown sugar
juice of 1 lemon
2 teaspoons crushed green peppercorns
6 tablespoons red wine
2 cloves garlic, crushed
2.5cm (1-inch) piece of green ginger root, minced or finely chopped
2 teaspoons French Dijon mustard
2 tablespoons sunflower oil

Place the meat in a dish. Combine all the marinade ingredients, pour over the meat and leave at room temperature, turning the meat every now and then and spooning marinade over it, for about seven hours.

Transfer the meat to a roasting tin, spreading the peppercorns, ginger and garlic over the top but discarding the rest of the marinade, and dribble over the oil. Roast in a very hot oven (475°F/240°C, gas mark 9) for 20 minutes. Leave to 'settle' for 10 minutes before carving into wafer-thin slices. Serve with minted new potatoes and crisply cooked French beans.

Beef teriyaki (see facing page)

Rendezvous of strawberries and kiwi fruit
(serves 6)

4 kiwi fruit
250g (8oz) strawberries
juice of 1 orange
2 tablespoons gin
castor sugar

Hull and thickly slice the strawberries. Peel and thinly slice the kiwi fruit into rounds. Arrange the kiwi fruit and strawberries in contrasting circles on a flat round dish. Pour over the orange juice and gin, and leave the fruit to macerate for at least one hour in refrigerator. Sprinkle over the sugar and serve chilled with some sweet biscuits.

Lady Carey Basset

A Norfolk Farmhouse Kitchen

I was most surprised to be invited to contribute to this book, because although I enjoy cooking and am quite good at dreaming up short cuts whilst warming my bottom against the Aga, I never thought I was *that* good a cook. In fact cooking can often be rather awkward because I share the Aga with my dogs, who insist upon their baskets being lined up against it; but they are quick to move out of the way when in danger.

My family home, Holkham Hall, is only two miles away, and I can just remember its huge old kitchen being in use; the public can now see it when the house is open during the summer. I thank God for modern appliances, and am glad we designed a fairly modern kitchen in our eighteenth-century farmhouse near the north Norfolk coast. There are no home-cured hams or sausages hanging from the ceiling, but we do boast a Miele dishwasher, big and small Magimixes and a deep-freeze. The latter is essential since I live in a male-orientated household with a husband and three sons, all of whom are thin but have vast appetites. The boys have many ravenous friends who invade the house at all times of the day and night, so I constantly need to be able to cater for the unexpected! When I'm on my own it's a relief to be able to crack a couple of eggs into a saucepan of simmering Crosse and Blackwell's consommé, which leaves only the spoon and pan to be washed up.

Our dining-room is seldom used, and I like to think the kitchen has a cosier, if somewhat smellier, atmosphere. Red shades on the candles serve a most important purpose: they hide the unwashed nightmares in the sink as well as my ever-increasing wrinkles. I'm a great believer in subdued lighting and music throughout dinner. The combination of the two often stops people from returning to the drawing-room, where the cushions are squashed, the ashtrays full, and the fire is invariably out.

We are very well off round here for free food and seafood. There are masses of

cockles and mussels, whose cooking juice I strain through muslin to avoid drinking mouthfuls of sand. In July we gather samphire on the sandy mud flats, and eat it like asparagus with hot melted butter; and shrimps we throw into very hot olive oil in which we've frizzled some whole peeled garlic cloves.

Fungi fill me with fear but I know what a Morel looks like: once seen never forgotten! They grow in a beech wood near here, and the location is my closely guarded secret as they are rare and difficult to find. I only wish my Border Terrier's nose was trained to sniff them out. Saffron Milk Caps grow under the Corsican Pine trees on Holkham beach; their top is saffron yellow which bruises to green, so they are not too difficult to identify. Their stalks should be cut off completely before they are braised in butter and enjoyed – crisp and fresh-flavoured. Parsley butter is good with them, or a cream sauce lightly flavoured with lemon peel and lovage.

My cousin, Robin Coombe, who lives nearby, produces luscious pink-fleshed trout from his Glaven Fish Farm. He breeds them in steel and concrete tanks, with the result that they don't have the muddy flavour sometimes associated with farm-reared trout.

Our lovely old-fashioned garden is open once a year in aid of The National Gardens Scheme, and we are lucky in having the best gardener in the world to look after it. Ben produces eggs, honey, flowers, fruit and herbs, can mend a bird's wing, and even finds time to teach the Sunday School children and to do some lay preaching.

When we have a glut of summer fruit I make a huge effort to make and freeze purées, sorbets and ice creams. There are not many sorbets that can be made all the year round, but pineapple is an exception, and looks pretty sitting in a fresh pineapple shell decorated with a sprig of mint. The best thing for freezing from the shooting season is mallard. I cook them for a maximum of 40 minutes, and put honey and fresh orange juice over them five minutes before serving.

Recently I spent a marvellous week with my sister, Sarah Walter, at Robert Carrier's seminar of cooking at Hintlesham Hall. We had enormous fun, and returned home full of new ideas. I now use far more wine and herbs in my dishes, and vegetables are cooked for only a few minutes in a minimum of fiercely boiling water before being refreshed quickly under the cold tap, drained, and tossed in hot butter. Finely sliced leeks, Brussels sprouts and cabbage are delicious done this way.

Top of my vegetable list are sorrel, spinach and Jerusalem artichokes. In fact I have a fetish for wind-producing artichoke soup. I boil the artichokes in their skins first, then squeeze out the flesh. The soup is even more delicious with roasted almonds sprinkled over the top, and a swirl of cream added just before serving. I don't mind telling readers about my habit of mixing juniper berries with black peppercorns (I only wish someone would invent a mill that went on longer than the ones I buy), but I am more reluctantly parting with my favourite recipe, Holkham Vegetable Pie. When I lived at Holkham after the war we all worked in the pottery which our mother started up about thirty years ago, and which I'm happy to say is still going strong. Wednesday was always Vegetable Pie day, and oh, the joy of scraping off the clay and paint and rushing into the dining-room, knowing that our wonderful Italian cook Tina had come up trumps again.

Mussel soup (serves 6)

600ml (1pt) mussels
600ml (1pt) shrimps, fresh or frozen
1 large onion, 1 carrot, 1 bay leaf
bunch of parsley
1 stick of celery
1 dessertspoon curry powder
1 small glass sherry
1 or 2 tablespoons single cream
2 tablespoons butter
flour to make a roux
a few drops of Tabasco
salt and pepper

Clean and scrub mussels after leaving them to soak in cold salted water for an hour or so. Peel shrimps. Put shrimp peelings (or some frozen ones) into a large saucepan with sliced carrot, ½ of a sliced onion, bay leaf and chopped parsley. Top with 900ml (1½pts) of cold water, cover and slowly bring to boil, simmer for 45 minutes and remove scum when necessary.

In another large saucepan put 1 tablespoon butter, chopped celery, chopped ½ of onion and cleaned mussels, cover and quickly bring to boil. Cook for 5 minutes, stirring occasionally. Remove mussels from shells and de-beard. Put with peeled (or rest of frozen) shrimps and reserve.

Now melt remaining butter, stir in flour and curry powder; when well blended and thickening, take off heat and strain in the shrimp and mussel broth from both saucepans. Stir well, add sherry, Tabasco, and lastly stir in cream, mussels and shrimps. Dust with chopped parsley.

Holkham vegetable pie (serves 4)

600ml (1pt) rich cheese sauce (fairly thin)
60g (2oz) butter
1 tablespoon olive oil
5 eggs
2 onions
3 large tomatoes
120g (4oz) or less of spaghetti
1 chicken stock cube
cream

Grease a pie dish with butter. Slice onions and fry slowly in butter and oil. Reserve. Boil eggs for 10 minutes, reserve in cold water. Boil spaghetti in salted water with a drop of oil until tender, rinse under hot tap, cover and reserve with buttered paper on top and put in low oven. Slice skinned tomatoes. Make cheese sauce and add chicken cube and cream. Shell and slice the eggs.

Layer the above ingredients in a pie dish starting and finishing with spaghetti. Pour cheese sauce over, and fork well in. Top with tomato slices, a sprinkling of cheese, butter flakes and a screw of pepper. Place in baking oven for 30 minutes until bubbling (400°F/200°C, gas mark 6).

Spinach goes well with this, and in the summer a green salad is nice.

Cold chocolate pudding (serves 4)

250g (8oz) plain chocolate
1 tablespoon water
5 eggs (separated)
120g (4oz) castor sugar
120g (4oz) butter (preferably unsalted)
250g (8oz) Boudoir biscuits or similar
1 cupful strong cold black coffee

Melt the chocolate in the water very gently and let it cool slightly. Stir in 5 egg yolks, castor sugar and melted butter. Whip egg whites very stiffly and fold into chocolate mixture.

Dip the biscuits very quickly into the strong cold coffee and press them upright round the sides of a tall soufflé dish, to which with luck they will stick. Pour in the chocolate mixture, cover with a piece of foil and a small plate and put a weight on top. Chill it overnight and serve with whipped cream piled on top.

Pineapple sorbet (serves 6)

1 medium-sized pineapple
300ml (½pt) water
180g (6oz) sugar
juice of 1 lemon
2 egg whites

Put the sugar and water in a saucepan, bring to the boil and boil over a high heat for 5 minutes. Leave to cool. Scoop out the flesh from a medium-sized fresh pineapple and process it until it is a purée (½pt). Add the lemon juice. Combine the syrup and the purée, and pour into shallow freezing trays. Freeze until the mixture has crystallised but is not completely solid. Whip the egg whites until stiff.

Break up the half-frozen ice and put it into the food processor, blend until mixture is just smooth, add beaten egg whites and then process again for just long enough to mix the ingredients evenly. Return the ice to the trays and freeze until solid.

For serving, scoop balls of the ice into the pineapple shell and decorate with a flower or a sprig of mint.

Catherine Beloe

A Year in the Life of a Farmhouse Kitchen

On a clear day you can see right from one end of the kitchen to the other – but that's not often.

The idea of living in a picturesque sixteenth-century thatched farmhouse on a smallholding in Gloucestershire may conjure up visions of a peaceful agrarian existence, but life inside the house, sadly, does not reflect the tranquillity and beauty of the surrounding countryside. Somehow the livestock, that's Sprightly and Buttercup, our two much-loved Jersey house cows, Mrs Piggy, a Gloucester Old Spot sow, lambs, geese, ducks and hens – all seem to enjoy a life of rural calm, which we would dearly love to emulate. From time to time they too enter the frantic world of the human being and join the party, uninvited, in the kitchen.

The most important feature of the kitchen is the Aga which not only keeps the whole house warm but also enables me to cook many things which I would not otherwise attempt. (One can also resuscitate runts in the bottom oven). It's not just a room where we cook and eat. It changes character constantly, one day resembling a disorganised butcher's shop strewn with meat and poultry, a week later littered with day-old chicks or newborn lambs; another month it could pass for a jam factory, or look like a display for Harvest Festival; but for at least ten months of the year it's in total chaos.

The finest months are January and February when it is fairly organised. Three gallons of rich creamy Jersey milk are brought over in buckets from the cowshed every morning and poured into Victorian chamber pots and put into the fridge to settle. Thick cream is skimmed off the top, and once a week this is made into butter. Surplus milk is either made into yogurt or fed to the animals. I've tried making cheeses and can produce a passable curd cheese, but otherwise there is a singular lack of success. Six ambitious Cotswold cheeses promoted themselves to the rank of

Family faggots (see p. 22)

Stilton and were totally inedible, and a Cheddar enjoyed a long spell as a football before finally being fed to the pig.

In March the kitchen really starts getting cluttered. The floor space around the Aga is taken up with orphan lamps being kept warm; they need milk four times a day while they are little, so we are constantly feeding them, washing out and re-filling their bottles, and tripping over them when trying to cook.

The geese, ducks, chickens and quail are all starting to lay in various secret places around the barns, and their eggs, if and when found, are brought into the kitchen for sorting. The sideboard is littered with eggs of all colours and sizes. Some are marked up and taken out to the incubator, and the rest are stacked in the egg tray for eating. Why is it that there are either too many eggs, or, just when we need some, none at all? When there are too many, there's a blitz and chocolate roulades are made for the deep-freeze.

March is also the time to start preparing the vegetable garden. The kitchen table is piled with trays of seedlings, forcing those who manage to stagger down to breakfast to eat it on their laps instead, until the threat of frost has passed and the plants can be put out into the garden.

By April, ducklings, goslings and quail are hatching out in the incubator, and boxes of chicks are brought into the warmth of the kitchen until they are strong enough to be let outside again to fend for themselves.

There are two public holidays in May, which means that we have more than our fair share of visitors. We are lucky enough to be able to rear our own 'baby' beef. A bull calf, born in September, suckle-reared and then killed at nine months old provides at least 100 lbs of beautifully tender meat, and because it's such good quality we normally just roast it plain. However, a friend who came to stay one weekend last May offered to take over, having perfected the art of Sunday lunch cuisine in order to avoid doing any farm work. The piece of beef which he smothered in mustard and then roasted in wine was quite delicious, and because of the tenderising effect that mustard has on meat, his is a very good method to use if you have to cook a rather tough piece of topside.

Some of the soft fruits in the garden are ready for picking in June, and baskets of strawberries and raspberries are brought into the kitchen for sorting. The very best are made into strawberry and raspberry tarts for eating straightaway, and about two dozen really perfect strawberries are painted with melted chocolate. When completely encased they are put into the fridge to set and then passed round with the coffee after a meal. It's surprising how few people can guess what the filling is. The second-grade fruit is packed and frozen for future use in mousses, fruit salads or for mixing into the home-made yogurt. Then the copper preserving pan is brought out, jam jars are resurrected, washed and put to dry in the bottom oven, and we spend hours making jam with the third-grade fruit. Jam-making day always seems to coincide with the hottest day of the year and, instead of being able to laze around in the sun, we spend hours leaning over the Aga stirring, skimming, testing, sweltering and *swearing* that next year we'll go out and buy the stuff.

By July the first batch of ducklings are ready to be dealt with. They are killed and then hung up by their feet on the washing line outside the kitchen because it's at just the right height for us to pluck them. We normally do about a dozen or so a day, and it's hard work plucking, singeing, drawing, dressing and finally bagging them up for the deep freeze. Fingers are numb, the yard is covered in feathers, and when it's all finished we reward ourselves by roasting the final duck in honey and perry for supper. The honey comes from our own bees, whose hive we brave each August.

September is my favourite month. All the work in the garden finally pays dividends, and the vegetables are brought into the kitchen to be prepared, blanched and frozen. The table groans under huge piles of broad and runner beans, spinach, sweet corn and cauliflowers. When these have been dealt with, the tomatoes are picked and boiled in large pans until reduced to a concentrated purée for storing in jars. Any tomatoes which haven't ripened by the end of the month are made into chutney. The whole house smells of vinegar as it bubbles away, and the pan comes out sparkling clean at the end of it.

Mrs Piggy produces a litter about twice a year. From the time the piglets are twelve weeks old they are fed on skimmed milk and barley meal until they are just a little over pork weight. Milk-fed pork is definitely worth trying; it's very sweet, with a thick layer of fat over the top, so it doesn't dry out when cooking. October is a good time to deal with the porkers. The offal is brought in to the kitchen to be made into faggots, and a brine is prepared and cooled down to await the arrival of the rest of the meat. A few days later, when the pork has finished hanging, it is cut up. At this point we take most of the belly joints and mince them, then marinade the mince in red wine and spices, and make yards of garlic sausages which hang above the Aga to dry out. They are then moved outside to a barn and left to mature for a couple of months. The heads are made into brawn, and the fat inside the pig is rendered down into lard in the bottom oven. A leg and a flitch are put into the brine tub to soak for a month or two, the rest of the meat is frozen, and, as a reward for our labours, we treat ourselves to a leg of pork roasted in milk, juniper berries and basil.

November is a lazy month for us. The garden is beyond redemption, the apples have all been picked, the plum wine and the perry have long since been made, and the deep-freeze is full. Our final task is to dispose of the lambs, since they have now run out of grass. Now is the time to invite our Sunday lunch cook down to stay again and if we threaten him hard enough with farm jobs to be done he'll cook us a leg of lamb in a green paste instead!

December, and the chickens are ready for killing. They are huge great things, reared in the manner of the famous *poulets de Bresse* on maize, molasses, wheat soaked in milk and left-over herbs and vegetables from the garden. They are hung for four days before being plucked and dressed. When cooked in butter, herbs and lemon they are tasty and succulent and have a marvellous golden colour to the skin.

So there it is, a year in the life of my kitchen. Most of the time it looks like a shambles, but on Christmas Eve, when the animals are shut away, the floor washed, the débris cleared, the table set and the candles lit, it almost looks as if you could *cook* in it!

Faggots (makes approx 32 faggots)

1.5kg (3lb) pig's liver
1 pig's heart
1 pig's spleen
125g (4oz) pig's lung (lights)
1 pig's caul
3 onions (large)
1 egg
sage, thyme, nutmeg
salt and black pepper
1 small loaf white bread (made into breadcrumbs)

Mince the liver, heart, spleen, and lights. Add the finely chopped onions, sage and thyme. Add the nutmeg, salt and pepper to taste.

Stir in enough breadcrumbs to soak up all the juices so that the mixture becomes the consistency of a stuffing.

Soak the caul in warm water and then spread it right out over an immaculately clean kitchen table.

When I get to this point the children come and help. I slide one hand under the caul; one child cuts the caul round my hand while the other drops a dollop of faggot mixture into my palm. I then fold the edges of the caul over the mixture in my palm to make a small parcel. If you don't have help, the scissors, spoon handle and both your hands get covered in faggot mixture.

The faggots should be put side by side in a baking tray, and water poured in until it reaches halfway up. Bake for 30 minutes in a moderate oven, then strain off the liquid (but retain it for gravy) and bake for a further 30 minutes.

Lamb in a green paste (serves 8)

2kg (4lb) leg of lamb
425ml (¾pt) fresh breadcrumbs
180g (6oz) butter
large bunch parsley
4–5 sprigs rosemary
1 sprig mint
a pinch of cumin
black pepper

Chop the parsley, 3 of the sprigs of rosemary, and the mint and mix with the breadcrumbs, cumin and black pepper. (I do this in the Magimix if I'm in a rush – which I always am.)

Melt the butter, stir it into the breadcrumbs and leave it for a few minutes. It will look a revolting khaki colour at this stage but don't be put off!

Wipe the leg of lamb with a damp cloth, put it on a trivet over a baking tray, and then slap the breadcrumb paste onto it, pressing it firmly into the meat, first on the underside and then on the top (extremely messy!). Give it a good 15-minute blast in a very hot oven (240°C/475°F, gas mark 9) before turning the heat right down to 180°/350°F, gas mark 4 for the next 1¼ hours (or 20 mins per lb). Cook it for longer if you prefer lamb well done.

When dishing it up, put the remaining sprigs of rosemary on top, and serve with carrots, sprouts and roast potatoes.

Pork in milk (serves 6–12, depending on size)

leg of pork
1 litre (2pts) of milk
4 large potatoes
1 onion
6 juniper berries
1 bay leaf
a few basil leaves
salt & black pepper
olive oil

Weigh the leg of pork. Score it deeply and in very thin strips. Preheat the oven to 230°C/450°F, gas mark 8. Rub olive oil over the surface and then really push the salt into the skin. Put it in the oven and cook for 30 minutes per pound. After 20 minutes turn the oven down to 160°C/325°F, gas mark 3.

Put the crushed juniper berries and folded bay leaf into the milk and set on a low heat to infuse for 20 minutes.

Slice the potatoes and onion wafer thin, and finely chop the basil leaves.

One hour before the end of cooking, take the joint out of the oven and out of the pan. Drain off the excess fat, and pour the milk through a strainer and into the pan. Add the potatoes, onion and basil, grind some black pepper over the top and stir. Put the pork back on top of the milk/potato mixture and cook for the final hour at 230°C/450°F, gas mark 8.

Serve with runner beans (I grow a stringless variety and cut them in chunks, not thin strips) and spinach just cooked for a minute.

Kitty Campion

Herbal Salad Making

Over three hundred years ago John Evelyn observed that he could 'by no means approve of the extravagant fancy of some who tell us that a Fool is as fit to be the gatherer of Sallets as a wise man.'

Salad-making is indeed an art. Almost anyone by following a recipe carefully can produce a good soup or a passable crumble but a salad requires more than mere diligence. It needs imagination, an artistic eye for colour and arrangement, and skill in the choosing and blending of ingredients. Don't let this intimidate you. A salad is one of those paradoxes, a simple dish which must be made with the utmost care. John Evelyn's advice about salad making is still sound: 'Every plant must bear its part, and they must fall into their places like the Notes in Music, and there must be nothing harsh or grating. And though admitting some discords (to distinguish and illustrate the rest) striking in the more sprightly and sometimes gentler Notes, reconcile all Disconances and melt them into an agreeable composition.'

The discords used 'to distinguish and illustrate the rest' might be fried bacon and mozzarella cheese with finely torn summer spinach, croûtons and toasted sunflower seeds with dandelion leaves; crunchy against soft – the perfect marriage.

Always consider the taste and texture as well as the colour of everything you want to include in your salad. Think too how to cut up each item. There are nearly always alternatives. Carrots, for example, can be diced, cut julienne, into rounds or half moons, grated, occasionally cooked and puréed or formed into delicate curls. Some fragile herbs, like chives and watercress leaves, are better cut with sharp scissors than a knife which will only pull them out of shape or bruise them so they turn black.

A herbalist at home

Lettuce, endive, young dandelion, sorrel and nettle leaves, and very tender spinach leaves should be used whole or, if the leaves are very large, they should be torn very gently by hand. They should never be shredded with a knife.

Melting a salad into ' an agreeable composition' very much depends on its arrangement. Should it be served tossed lightly together in a large bowl, in separate side bowls, or on oval platter in circles, or as the Greeks do in layers on a plate? The Elizabethans took great pride in their 'crowned sallets' which were used as the centre-piece on their banqueting tables. They were towering edifices which took many hours to construct. The centre-piece was often a castle of paste with towers and ramparts of carrots, turnips and beet, the courtyard garden was planted with small herbs and flowers, and steps surrounding the whole were made of paste, and each one would have been spread with a different salad. Not that I'm suggesting anything as elaborate as this, but do remember that salads make magnificent centre-pieces. Don't be brow-beaten by French *haute cuisine* into believing that only a grandly decorated slab of meat or fish will do. Comfort yourself with these Buddhist instructions to an aspiring cook which have often bolstered my courage when I'm about to present a salad as a meal in itself to critical, meat-loving friends: 'If one is moved by things and people, one is also able to move them. The pure actions of the cook come forth from his realisation of the unity of all things and beings, and by seeing clearly into the minds and hearts of others, from a cabbage he must be able to produce a sixteen-foot Buddha.'

Which reminds me of a memorable meal where I created not a sixteen-foot Buddha but something fairly close. I used a magnificent fully blown savoy cabbage as a centre-piece, and placed bowls of simple crudités and more complicated mixtures of marinaded mushrooms with coriander, and cherry tomatoes stuffed with smoked oysters, in the pockets of the leaves. I hollowed out the top of the cabbage slightly and filled it with bowls of soft herb jellies, mint chutney, herb salad dressings and dips. Nothing was wasted. The cabbage afterwards made an excellent soup.

Sixteenth- and seventeenth-century cook books testify that it was not at all unusual to have as many as thirty ingredients in one salad which would include, apart from the lettuce and other salad herbs commonly used today, almonds, marrows, barberries (the fruit of the common berberis), broom-buds (as substitutes for capers), pickled ash-keys, elder-buds, walnuts, purslane stalks, currants, raisins, samphire (which used to grow abundantly in many places around the coast of Britain), strawberry leaves, ox-eye daisy leaves, lemon and orange peel, nasturtiums, rocket, borage, and all sorts of fresh and candied flowers. John Parkinson suggested another charming salad addition: 'The kernals or seed (of oranges) being cast into the ground in the spring time, will quickly grow up . . . and when they are of a finger length height being plucked up, and put among salads, will give them a marvellous fine aromatic or spicy taste, very acceptable.'

So be adventurous with your salad ingredients. Try Florence fennel which has a distinct flavour, celeriac which, as its name suggests, tastes of celery but doesn't plague one with those annoying stringy bits which stick between one's teeth, domestic sorrel which is less bitter than the wild plant, kohlrabi, tender yarrow leaves, sweet cicely, lovage which tastes like peppery celery with a hint of parsley in it, young comfrey leaves, borage, tender young nettles and all the flower leaves and petals of which the Elizabethans were so fond. You will transform your salad into a celebration!

Raw green and leafy vegetables are bursting with vitamins and valuable mineral salts, most of which are lost when they are cooked. If you must cook them I would suggest the Chinese stir-fried method or a vegetable steamer. In this way most of the goodness will be retained. The dark outer leaves of green vegetables are two to five times richer in vitamins than their bleached hearts which only contain traces of vitamin A. This is especially true of herbs like nettles, endives, yarrow, parsley and dandelion. Sadly, parsley is all too often used simply as a decoration, and only the Arabs continue to use it in large quantities as the basis of salads, yet it is crammed with vitamin A and is three times richer in vitamin C than oranges. Dandelion leaves contain four times more vitamin C than lettuce, are rich in potassium, and richer in iron than spinach.

The most important rules for the salad maker are as follows. All ingredients should be as fresh as possible. In the life of the more delicate salad plants a few hours out of the ground is half a life-time. Freshness may be impractical for the city dweller, but if you have to store salad ingredients wash them quickly and gently as soon as you can and keep them crisp and cold. Prolonged soaking in water merely leaches them of their valuable salts. This is particularly true of celery and endive. If fresh herbs must be stored, wash them quickly, shake them dry and store them in the fridge in airtight plastic containers. Be very careful not to bruise salad stuffs. When you are instructed to toss a salad this does not call for a modified game of rugby! The French phrase *'fatiguer la salade'* does not mean mutilate the salad by wearing it down with sharp spoons and an aggressive arm. The process should be more like gently folding egg whites into cream.

In Elizabethan times all green leafy vegetables were loosely categorised as salad herbs along with the plants we call herbs today. Elizabethan cooks were never tediously cautioned to use salad herbs or herbs themselves in a miserly fashion as is so often the sermonising theme of cook books today. Blends and quantities were left to the cook's discretion and experience. Nor did herbalists burden themselves with weighing scales. They simply used their hands and eyes as measures, as in this recipe from *The Good housewife's Jewell*, 1585: 'To Make a Sallet of All Kinde of Hearbs: Take your hearbs and pick them very fine with faire water and pick your flowers by themselves and wash them all cleane and swing them in a dish, mingle them with Cowcumbres or Lemmons payred and sliced and scrape sugar and put in ginger and oyle and throw the flowers on top of the sallet.'

So be generous or not with herbs and salad stuffs as your own taste dictates. You will find basil pungent, and a couple of fresh leaves will usually be enough. Marjoram is less so, and in a Greek salad I am usually quite generous with it. Cicely, on the other hand, with its delicately sweet anise-flavour can be used liberally. I use the lacy leaves, which feel exquisitely silky, as a platter on which I lay my strawberries and cucumber salad. Take advantage of the several varieties of each herb. For example, don't neglect the milder fragrant applemint, the cooling menthol peppermint, and the delicious smelling bergamot mint which is so reminiscent of eau-de-cologne. The beauty of salad stuffs, vegetables and herbs is that they force you to drift with the seasons. The journey should be an instructive one. The hardy aromatic herbs will suggest themselves in winter, together with the dried seeds you may have gathered and stored in the autumn. My various mints, thymes and sage continue to offer themselves past Christmas. My parsley, marjoram and borage, sheltered by the garden wall, struggle on bravely until November. Enjoy the abundance of the summer herbs like basil, chives, balm and summer savory and all the flowers while you can.

The Elizabethans scattered some of the best edible flowers like borage, sageflowers, bergamot, anchusa, marigolds, rosemary flowers, lavender, rose petals and nasturtiums over their summer salads. In preparation for the winter they preserved flowers, especially cowslips and clove gillyflowers of which they were particularly fond, packed in layers of sugar in gallipots which were then topped up with vinegar. Evelyn believed that fresh flowers gave 'a more palatable relish' to salads if they were first infused in vinegar, but I have found that vinegar makes them look soggy and somewhat colourless. Sometimes they added candied flowers to winter salads, but I feel these are more suitable for our fruit salads, and make unique dessert decorations.

Flowers, either whole petals or mixed and finely chopped, certainly add a carnival air to a salad. Complement whatever salad you decide to use with a matching or appropriate vinegar. Use lavender vinegar with lavender flowers or elderflower vinegar which blends nicely with cowslips. Always add your flower petals after you have added the dressing and tossed the salad, otherwise they will either become bruised in the tossing or absorb the oil and start to drop. Make sure with flowers, as with all your other salad stuffs, that they are well-washed under running water and thoroughly drained. Handle them gently and if using large flowers, like marigolds, use the petals only, detaching them by pulling them away from the centre. Discard the calyxes of flowers like borage, which have an unpalatably furry texture, or nasturtiums and sweet peas, which taste bitter.

Celebration salad

½kg (1lb) French green beans
360g (12oz) artichoke hearts, sliced crossways
¼kg (½lb) marinaded button mushrooms
1 tart green apple, peeled, cored and diced

Green herb mayonnaise
15ml (1 tablespoon) chopped parsley and lemon balm
2½ml (½ teaspoon) mixed marjoram and lovage
300ml (½pt) thick mayonnaise

The day before you want this salad wipe the mushrooms clean, slice them into thick pieces and pour over a marinade of hot red wine herb vinegar. Cover and set aside for 24 hours. Cook the green beans in a vegetable steamer until just tender, then drain, quickly immerse in cold water to cool, and drain again. Strain the mushrooms and mix them in a large bowl with the beans, artichoke hearts and apple.

Make the green herb mayonnaise by putting the chopped parsley and lemon balm, with the mixed marjoram and lovage, into a liquidiser with the thick mayonnaise. Blend. It will be a beatiful green colour. Coat everything with this mayonnaise. Arrange the flowers in an intricate design on the top or scatter them with gay abandon. It's up to you. Use the flowers as an expression of how you feel! Serve immediately.

Mirabel Cecil

A Feast for Children

There is no doubt that cooking for children is a very different art from cooking for grown-ups. Children only recognise two culinary schools, the 'yukky' and the 'yummy'. Their diagnosis is rapid – one taste and a beam of pleasure, or a caricature of horror and revulsion crosses their faces. Accordingly they either eat three helpings at speed or spend half an hour pushing the offending morsels round their plates, writhing the while as if they are being poisoned.

Even more than adults, children are divided into the 'I don't like it, what is it?' school, and those willing to taste anything once. When I took my three children to France for the first time, two of them ate *moules marinières*, snails and smelly cheese, the third only wanted fish and chips and ice cream – in fact, the standard fare of home.

Children like 'fast food'. A two-minute wait is acceptable; 20 minutes means table-banging and wails of starvation (this is the opposite of cooking for the elderly who like to have everything cooked for ages, and to eat it slowly).

I was very complimented when my bachelor brother, whose favourite nourishment is *pâté de foie gras* washed down with champagne, sat at my kitchen table and said admiringly, 'Your fast food is really good', as I tossed pancakes and served them up at speed. After a decade of motherhood I could easily become a short-order chef in an

Hallowe'en party

American restaurant. 'Fast food' is not to be confused with 'junk food'. Home-made hamburgers, for instance, are both nourishing and swift to make.

What has transformed nursery food since my childhood, for cook and consumer, is the amount of ready-made food available, from fish fingers to yogurt. Many of these can be made more nourishing: for instance, packet jellies can be made up with real fruit juice, and oversweet yogurts can be extended with home-made plain yogurt.

Two essential aids to cooking for children are food colours and cutters. Food colours take children's minds off what they are eating; they will consume something they profess to hate, such as cauliflower cheese, if a few drops of purple or yellow are added. Letter and number cake-moulds and cutters help to make food fun for children. My brother-in-law, Angelo Hornak, an excellent and imaginative cook, keeps a regiment of pizza soldiers in his freezer.

For school holidays ice-lolly moulds are a good investment; you can thus avoid buying commercial lollies and make your own using real fruit juice. Another good idea is home-made milk shakes using milk, ice cream and any of the extras suggested below.

Children, quite rightly, see cooking as an extension of playing. The rather pretentious phrase 'creative cooking' really does apply to them: they love to create something from diverse raw ingredients. From an early age both boys and girls should be encouraged to cook – and to clear up afterwards. One of the most successful recipes my children started with is for cheese straws; these need only a few minutes' cooking time, so they can see the results quickly (most important) and have the additional pleasure of being able to offer their handiwork round.

What children enjoy best of all are 'occasions'. They have a great sense of celebration, are delighted with even a simple birthday cake, and horrified by the absence of one. On one of my birthdays the children were so shocked that my husband had forgotten the event altogether that my son, aged six, said he would make me a birthday cake, whilst my daughter, aged four, hurried off down the village street to invite a few neighbours to tea. We made an uncooked chocolate and orange cake, which demands much satisfying crushing of biscuits and melting of chocolate.

If you can dress food up to suit an occasion it will be a sure success. Small boys love Hallowe'en for the excuse it provides to rush about shrieking in sheets. 'Please come looking horrible' said the invitation – which was in the shape of a bat – to a most successful Hallowe'en party my son went to. His little friend's mother greeted guests in a fetching coiffure of ringlets coiled about with rubber snakes. The food was *en suite*: everything had names of extreme revoltingness which must have taken many happy hours to dream up. A greeen and yellow jelly with half a black grape on top was 'Cyclop's Eye', strawberry ice cream with raspberry sauce running down it was 'Dracula's Nosebleed', peanuts were 'Witches' Teeth', crisps 'Giants' Toenails', and sausages 'Goblins' Fingers'. According to the hostess, all of this was eaten with relish, which tells us much about children's approach to food. Can anyone suggest what I might rechristen cabbage in order to persuade my children to eat it? Mermaid's bedclothes, perhaps?

Home-made milk shake

300ml (½pt) milk
4 tablespoons ice cream

Put all the milk and half the ice cream into a large screw-top jar. Screw the lid on tightly and hand the jar to a child to shake, until the contents are thick and frothy. For a stronger flavour add a dash of the ice cream flavour – for instance, fruit syrup. Pour the contents into long glasses; top with the remainder of the ice cream. Drink through a straw if liked.

Uncooked chocolate and orange cake

310–375g (10–12oz) biscuits (digestives are suitable)
2 tablespoons each of cocoa powder, chocolate
  spread, and golden syrup
60g (2oz) butter or margarine
a handful of glacé cherries, chopped
1 or 2 oranges

Melt the butter or margarine, then add the golden syrup. When this is nicely sticky add the cocoa powder gradually and then the chocolate spread. While this gooey mess is slowly melting crush the biscuits in a bag with a rolling pin. Grease a shallow cake tin, such as a sponge tin.

Tip the crushed biscuits into a mixing bowl; pour over the chocolate sauce; add the glacé cherries and stir all well together. Now add as much of the juice of the orange as will leaven the richness of the cake without making it sloppy – about 2 dessertspoonfuls. Press the cake into the tin and give the mixing bowl to a child to scrape.

Put the cake in the refrigerator to set while you make an orange water-icing with the remaining juice and the grated rind of the orange. Pour this over the cake. When it is firm, decorate as appropriate. It is best kept chilled.

Orange icing (for uncooked chocolate and orange cake)

250g (8oz) icing sugar
4 dessertspoons (approx) orange juice
grated rind of ½ an orange

Sift the icing sugar into a mixing bowl; mix in the orange juice with a fork until there are no lumps left. Add the grated rind. The icing should be thick and creamy by now – if you think it too thick, add some more orange juice or a little water to thin.

Smear the icing over the cake as evenly as possible.

Pizza people

Have ready either a gingerbread-man cutter, or 2 circular cutters, one small (for heads) the other larger (for bodies), grease one large or two small baking trays.

Take one packet of bread mix; make it up as directed on the packet and when you have kneaded the dough for a few minutes, instead of shaping it into loaves, roll it out on a floured board until about 6mm (¼ inch) thick. Then cut it into shapes: in the absence of a gingerbread-man cutter, I cut small circles for heads and larger ones for bodies and place them one on top of the other, which seems to work. Place these in the required order on the baking tray(s) and leave them to rise for 15–20 minutes, covered with a damp cloth, in a warm place. Turn the oven on to 180°C/350°F, gas mark 4 to warm up, and make the topping.

Topping ingredients
½ onion, finely chopped
3 or 4 rashers streaky bacon
1 tin of tomatoes
125g (4oz) cheese, such as Cheddar
tomato purée (optional)

Sweat the finely chopped onion in a frying pan over a low heat. While it is cooking chop the bacon and remove rinds. Add the bacon to the onion and cook. Open the tin of tomatoes and chop them roughly. Add them to the other ingredients in the pan with a squirt from the tomato purée tube. Add salt and pepper with discretion. Stir. Leave to cook gently while you grate the cheese.

By this time the dough should have risen, though this will not be particularly perceptible. Don't worry. Decorate the creatures by lifting the topping mixture with a slatted spoon from the pan and placing it on the 'bodies'. I leave the 'heads' undecorated except for a salami smile, (to be eaten), and peppercorn eyes and noses, (not to be eaten). Sprinkle some grated cheese over each body, reserving some for later use.

Put the trays into the pre-heated oven and bake for 20–25 minutes, looking at them once in case the trays need turning round. To serve, slide the pizza people onto a plate and let each child use imagination to decorate them further with grated cheese for 'hair' and cheese cut into sticks for arms and legs. I imagine this could be done with pastry, using slices of cooking apples and raisins, or jam and nuts for the topping.

The Countess of Chichester

Town and Country Entertaining

Living in the country with a good vegetable garden and a farm, we try to be as self-sufficient as possible, not only for the satisfaction it brings, but also because I find marketing a terrible chore and feel conscience-stricken when I have to buy food.

We usually stay about two nights a week in London and often go with a few friends to the theatre or opera. Rather than being faced at a late hour with choosing from a menu, ordering, tired waiters, delays and sometimes being made to feel uneasy or hurried, we find it more fun and more relaxing to eat at home – it's also cheaper. When in London, I have neither the time nor the inclination to spend hours in the kitchen, and in any case our country kitchen is better equipped. So we plan a dinner than can be packed into a large cardboard box and taken to London in the boot of the car. The food to be heated is unloaded straight into the warming drawer, and the rest is put onto the dining-room table. Upon our return with guests, I just light the candles and bring out the hot food, so I am quite free to enjoy myself.

As a first course I sometimes give smoked eels, skinned and filleted and prettily laid out, surrounded with a generous quantity of lemon wedges and parsley. We have our own eel stage, and in the Autumn when we have caught a batch of twelve or fifteen we take them to be smoked. Unfortunately we have found those little homesmoking machines inadequate, as a good plump eel needs several days' slow smoking to taste right. I serve this with my 'healthy bread', so called because it contains no animal fat but plenty of roughage and Vitamin B. We make the flour for it by grinding our own wheat in the electric coffee grinder. It is quite delicious though rather crumbly.

As a main course I have a pheasant dish which is unusual and mouthwateringly good. The pheasant is cooked in a creamy sauce with a light fluffy topping. While you are in the theatre it will wait happily for you, warming gently. I tend to serve

Back from the shoot

pheasant in London rather than in the country where lots of our shooting friends find them rather over-familiar by the middle of the season.

Although reheating vegetables is generally frowned upon, I think that carrots Vichy and a spinach ring do not deteriorate if covered tightly with tinfoil lined with greaseproof paper, and they go well with the pheasant in terms of colour, texture and taste.

A light, clean end to this repast is blackcurrant and wine jelly with cassis cream. Sometimes I serve it with a rather good cookie, which even the more diet-conscious can't resist nibbling with coffee.

In winter in the country, shooting lunches are a fairly regular event and I have, I hope, gradually learnt the main requirement, namely to satisfy voracious appetites quickly, but with style. Usually we have eight guns, and, with wives and children invited too, we normally have around sixteen to feed. As winter days are short, speed is all-important. Lunch for me is accompanied by a slight feeling of anxiety that either it will be dark before the last drive, or the beaters will be kept waiting, unless I get everyone fed fast enough. Our eating time is always reduced by extra minutes spent trying to pick a bird before coming in and even more time lost struggling before and afterwards with muddy boots and accompanying paraphernalia. There is time for everyone to get around the fire and have a drink (two if they are quick) before going in to lunch.

I begin by giving a thick, hearty, hot soup made from a great mixed stock of bones and vegetables and served with home-made brown bread rolls, again made with our own flour. We have our own beef, so I take a large piece of topside or silverside to make a pot roast, which I do by cooking the meat very slowly on a bed of assorted root vegetables with a little red wine, beef stock, herbs and seasonings. The juices are reduced to make a sauce. I cut it thinly and arrange the slices on a long dish, pouring the sauce over it. Around the edge I pipe, in alternate billows, a sprout purée mixed with mashed potatoes, and a beetroot purée and mashed potatoes, also mixed together. We make sure these vegetable mixtures are well seasoned with salt and pepper, and beat in plenty of butter, making certain there are no lumps. This manner of serving the vegetables has several advantages. It goes well with the meat, keeps the sauce on the dish, helps to soak it up as you eat, and means that each dish has everything on it, meat, vegetables and potatoes, therefore only needing to be passed to each person once, thus saving more time. Also it looks spectacular. Second helpings are *de rigueur* before going on to the pudding!

We have a lot of apples and, most years, good walnuts; so, as meringues seem to be popular with elderly gentlemen and children, we often give Apple Snowballs at shoots, on half-terms and at Christmas-time. The meringue can be piled cone-shaped over each apple and decorated with red and black currants and a few pralined beech nuts. Beech nuts are a dreadful fiddle to prepare but I think it is worth doing a few every autumn as they are so good, either toasted with salt to have with drinks, or made into a praline to go on puddings. For Apple Snowballs I just peel and core cooking apples, fill each cavity with chopped walnuts and stale cake crumbs moistened with our farm honey, and brush them with melted butter. They are then baked for about 35 minutes in a moderate oven. When they are cool I coat them with a meringue mixture, sprinkle them with sugar and leave them in the bottom of the Aga till they are crisp and golden, and until they are needed, as they can be left there without coming to any harm. I serve them with cream.

After this and with the coffee we pass around cherry brandy and home-made sloe gin. Somehow sixteen people always manage to get through this three-course lunch within an hour with no outward appearance of rush!

Healthy bread (makes about 12 slices)

250g (8oz) margarine
180g (6oz) wholemeal flour (home-ground)
½ teaspoon salt
3 teaspoons baking powder
water to mix

Grease a swiss-roll tin and line the base with greased greaseproof paper. Cream the margarine until light, then mix in the dry ingredients with enough water to form a stiff dough. Spread it evenly in the tin and brush generously with beaten egg. Sprinkle with coarsely ground wheat and bake in a preheated oven at 180°C/350°F, gas mark 4 for 15 minutes until risen and brown. When cool, turn out and store in an airtight tin.

Pheasant under a toasted top (serves 4)

1 pheasant, cooked and divided into large pieces

Velouté sauce
15g (½oz) butter
15g (½oz) flour
300ml (½pt) chicken or other light stock
3 tablespoons cream
a few drops of lemon juice
salt and pepper

4 tablespoons porridge oats, fried in butter until golden
300ml (½pt) cream, less 3 tablespoons for velouté sauce
grated rind of a lemon
salt and pepper
½ teaspoon made mustard
2 egg whites

Arrange cooked pheasant in a fireproof dish and pour the velouté sauce over it. Beat the remainder of the cream until stiff and add the grated lemon rind, salt, pepper and mustard to it. Beat the egg whites until they form peaks and fold them into the cream. Spread the mixture over the pheasant. Sprinkle with the oats and cook in a preheated oven at 175°C/350°F, gas mark 4 for about 20 minutes or until golden. This dish may be slowly reheated later.

Spinach ring with carrots Vichy

2 cups cooked chopped spinach
4 tablespoons thick cream
4 eggs
a few drops of onion juice
2 tablespoons melted butter
1½ teaspoons salt
½ teaspoon white pepper
dash of cayenne pepper

Carrots (cleaned and sliced as thinly as possible into discs)
1 or 2 lumps sugar, according to the quantity of carrots
a large lump of butter
salt
pepper
chopped parsley

Beat eggs and add all the ingredients for the spinach ring into them and mix well. Turn this into a well-buttered ring mould. Set the mould in a pan of hot water and bake at 150°C/300°F, gas mark 2 until firm, about 30 minutes. Turn out very carefully.

Fill the centre and surround the edge with carrots which you have cooked by putting a very little water into a heavy saucepan and bringing it to the boil. When it is boiling add the sugar, the butter and the carrots. Cook with the pan covered until the carrots are almost done, then remove the lid, increase the heat and boil off the liquid, stirring all the time to avoid burning and to allow the carrots to become slightly browned. Season with salt and pepper and add the parsley.

Pot roast, apple snowballs, and healthy bread

Pot roast (serves 10 people)

2kg (4lb) topside or brisket of beef (tied up neatly)
4 large onions (peeled and cut into strips)
2 large parsnips (peeled and cut into strips)
2 sticks celery, sliced
1 celeriac, diced
1 small turnip or swede
250g (½lb) field mushrooms, sliced
500g (1lb) tomatoes, peeled, seeded and chopped
4 streaky bacon rashers, with rinds removed and cut into strips
a few home-pickled walnuts and juice
1 bay leaf
parsley stalks and chopped leaves
1 bouquet garni
beef stock and red wine
2 tablespoons flour
a little dripping
salt and pepper

Melt the dripping in a large thick-bottomed casserole. When hot, brown the trussed piece of beef on all sides to seal. Remove and set on one side. Put in the bacon pieces, and when slightly cooked, add the remainder of the vegetables, except the tomatoes and mushrooms, walnuts and herbs. Cook and stir until they are lightly browned, then sprinkle in the flour and stir it until it absorbs the fat. Cook it a little further, then gradually pour in the wine and stock, stirring constantly, to make a thin sauce. Now add the tomatoes, mushrooms, pickled walnuts and juice, also the herbs and seasonings. Replace the beef in the casserole, cover it and put it in the bottom of a slow oven, 150°C/300°F, gas mark 2 for about 3 hours or until tender.

While this is cooking, boil and mash 1kg (2lb) potatoes, 500g (1lb) beetroot and 500g (1lb) spinach or other green vegetable, each cooked and puréed separately. Mix half the potatoes with the beetroot purée and the other half with the green purée. Into both mixtures beat butter and season. Pipe these mixtures in alternate castles around the edge of a large serving dish.

When the meat has cooled slightly, remove it from the casserole and slice it fairly thickly, arranging the slices on the piped dish. Strain the vegetables from the casserole and make a border with them around the meat. Then remove the bay leaf, parsley stalks and bouquet garni from the juice and reduce it to a suitable thickness by fast boiling. Check seasonings and pour it over the meat. Before serving, sprinkle it with chopped parsley.

Blackcurrant and wine jelly (serves 8)

2 tablespoons gelatine
⅓ cup water
3¼ cups sweetened blackcurrant juice (made from straining stewed fresh or frozen blackcurrants)
1 cup red wine
½ cup chopped walnuts
2 tablespoons crème de cassis
300ml (½pt) whipping cream

Soak the gelatine in the water. Boil 1 cup of sweetened blackcurrant juice and dissolve the softened gelatine in it. When it is properly dissolved add the remaining 2¼ cups of cold juice and the red wine. When the jelly begins to thicken, fold in the walnuts. Serve with lightly beaten cream to which you have added the cassis. These proportions will make a soft jelly of very good consistency to serve from a bowl or individual sorbet glasses. It will not form a mould and is not nearly so good if made too stiff.

Cookies for the jelly

180g (6oz) butter
60g (2oz) icing sugar
60g (2oz) cornflour
120g (4oz) plain flour
grated rind of a large orange
chopped nuts if desired
a few drops vanilla essence

Cream together the butter, sugar and grated rind. Mix in the two flours and add a few drops of vanilla essence. You can add a quantity of chopped nuts if you like. Make this dough into a roll, wrap it in foil, and chill in the refrigerator until firm.

Whenever you require some fresh cookies, cut a piece off the roll, roll it in sugar to coat the outside, then slice it into 6mm (¼-inch) thick discs and place, well separated, on a greased baking sheet. Bake in an oven preheated to 190°C/375°F, gas mark 5 until pale golden, about 10 minutes.

These biscuits are quite brittle, so allow them to cool before removing them from the tray. In order to eat them very fresh, you can keep the roll in the refrigerator and only slice off and bake a small quantity at a time, as you need them.

Lady Silvia Combe

Grandchildren's Lunch

My greatest delight nowadays is to give a Sunday lunch for as many of my six grandchildren as I can muster. I always cook as much as I can for these occasions on the previous day, so that all I have to do on Sunday morning after church is to remove the dishes from the fridge and warming cupboard, take the potatoes from the Aga, and relax and enjoy their company.

My kitchen has been the focal point of the house's activities since we came here in 1945. It has also been the scene of many parties and celebrations, perhaps the most momentous being the impromptu supper we organised on VE day. We had invited our nearest neighbours – petrol for parties being non-existent – and friends from the neighbouring airfield. All day long the airmen had been circling above the house, dropping streams of silver paper which we instantly appropriated for decorations. It was only that night that we learned that these so-called 'windows' had been used to fox the Germans into thinking that a huge air-raid was to be launched miles from where the actual raid was planned, the paper showing up on the screen as aircraft. The joyous evening ended with singing and dancing, and as rationing was still very much in force, we relied on our own hens and the kitchen garden. I remember egg cutlets, a vegetarian dish called 'Aunt Nellie's Pie', and *pain perdu*, bread soaked in vanilla milk, smothered in clarified butter, fried and served with whipped cream.

I inherited my most prized possession, a large and wonderfully solid kitchen table, from an aunt after all our furniture had been blitzed during the war. The original hand pump, wall oven and washing copper still remain alongside all the modern appliances that I couldn't do without. How past generations managed I don't know, although it can't have been too difficult for my grandmother, whose contribution to her kitchen I remember studying as a child. She would summon her cook at 10.30 every morning, and interview her in her 'boudoir', either agreeing with the day's menu, or substituting another.

That was the sum total of her contribution to the day's gargantuan meals, beginning with a huge breakfast with some ten dishes to choose from, and followed by a three-course lunch, tea and a five-course dinner. My grandfather was a gourmet in his own way and indulged in some pretty strange tastes. One of his favourite breakfast dishes was the velvet off the deer's antlers which had been shed in the park. To me it always looked and tasted like black leather! Another favourite was boiled cockles which we would have had to gather for him from the beach in the afternoon, in order that he should have them fresh for dinner.

My grandfather lived to be a hale and hearty 94-year-old, and attributed his rude health to exercise, the bracing Norfolk air, and his habit of eating raw onions whenever he went shooting – which he did rather often.

I don't think my grandchildren will have such an intersting range of eccentricities to talk about in years to come, but there is an apocryphal story about my dislike of waste which my children are always reminding me of. After one Christmas lunch I hung the turkey carcase out for the birds to enjoy, until some unexpected guests suddenly turned up for Boxing Day lunch, whereupon I am said to have retrieved it in order to make soup!

Now that the more formal many-coursed meals of past generations have largely been dispensed with, I am more than happy to cook my grandchildren their favourite Sunday lunch of lasagne and *pain de choux Bruxelles*, followed by Dutch apple charlotte and perhaps a banana or blackcurrant ice cream.

Pain de choux Bruxelles (serves 8)

700g (1½lb) Brussels sprouts
45g (1½oz) fresh breadcrumbs soaked in a wineglassful of milk
45g (1½oz) butter
1 egg yolk
(1½ gills) béchamel sauce
nutmeg

Boil sprouts, drain and press in small handfuls to extract water. Liquidise, then put purée in a pan with the butter. Mix, adding salt, pepper and a grate of nutmeg. Stir well on a low fire in order to melt the butter, then add soaked, sieved bread, and the egg yolk. Readjust the seasoning. Put it in the fridge overnight, turn into a buttered mould, and cook in a bain-marie in the oven for 40 minutes (375°F/180°C, gas mark 4). Turn out and pour béchamel sauce over it before serving.

Dutch apple charlotte (serves 8)

1kg (2lb) cooking apples
2–3 tablespoons water
60g (2oz) castor sugar
finely grated rind of ½ a lemon

Crumb mixture
120g (4oz) fresh white or brown breadcrumbs
120g (4oz) castor sugar
150g (5oz) butter

Peel, core and slice apples. Place them in a saucepan with the water. Cover with a lid and cook very gently for about 30 minutes, stirring occasionally, until the apples are soft. Draw the pan off the heat and stir in sugar and lemon rind.

Melt the butter in a large frying pan, add the mixed crumbs and sugar and cook gently, stirring occasionally until golden brown.

Combine layers of crumb and sweetened apple purée in a buttered 2-pint baking dish beginning and ending with layers of crumb. Keep in fridge overnight and, the next day, place in the centre of a moderate oven and bake for 30 minutes. Serve with cream.

Kate Corbett-Winder

A Welsh Farmhouse Weekend

As a single girl working in London, my life consisted of a series of dinner parties made up of last-minute menus decided by the time, money and energy I had available. Moving to mid-Wales to marry my farmer husband William has meant those single dinners have grown into whole weekends. After a year of intensive weekend entertaining (we've counted over sixty names in the visitors' book) I have learnt from experience to prepare as many meals as possible in advance, since I put friends before food and don't want to spend the whole weekend in the kitchen feeling like a martyred food-processor.

Our farmhouse isn't enormous, so the most comfortable number of guests is two or three. Some weekends we may expand to a daring six people for dinner on Saturday, but rarely any more! As these visits are almost a weekly event, my cooking is kept simple and fairly economical. I avoid any recipes needing last-minute attention, or complicated dishes that are ruined unless eaten at a specific time, because our kitchen equipment is not geared to such precision cooking. With a Rayburn, temperature control can never be completely reliable, so I stick to dishes that look after themselves, like slow casseroles and baked vegetables.

I consider my deep-freeze to be a trusty but extra-hungry guest, so when I am cooking I try to muster the time and ingredients to treat it accordingly. I also try to keep all plans fluid – always helpful when weekenders arrive bearing food parcels of runny cheeses and fresh pasta only fit for immediate consumption!

Shopping in small country towns can be frustrating if you have fixed ideas of what to cook before setting out. The quality and quantity of fresh supplies are unpredictable, so it is pointless to plan a meal that depends on a carton of sour cream or buttermilk, or on aubergines, peppers or avocados – all the things one took for granted in London. Instead, I dive into our local health shop for pulses, and often incorporate flageolets, haricots and kidney beans into salads and warming winter soups.

Friday nights can be a culinary disaster. I feel friends deserve a welcoming hot dinner as a reward for driving so far, but my efforts are often in vain. Some people arrive simply too tired or too late to eat anything, others admit sheepishly that they were hungerstruck in the middle of Gloucestershire and ate on the way, so my Friday night dinners are always moveable feasts. My faithful standby is a steak, kidney and mushroom casserole, served with baked potatoes, which can be fried for breakfast if unwanted, and a crisp green salad. Another useful dish is a sausage puff pie, served with a home-made hot tomato sauce. It can be eaten straight from the oven, or lukewarm, or cold the next day.

As farmers still have to work at weekends, breakfast is usually eaten in overlapping sittings in the kitchen. Invariably, people who swear they never touch it change their minds, and, using the country air as an excuse, tuck into porridge, eggs and bacon, and toast and marmalade.

Saturday lunch is more of a picnic: a carrot, watercress or onion soup from the freezer, hot bread, chicken liver or smoked mackerel pâté made the day before in the Magimix, and a filling salad of kidney beans, chopped celery, parsley and fried crispy bacon dressed with a garlic vinaigrette, followed by cheese and fruit.

Saturday night is definitely the culinary highspot of the weekend. A typical menu with little last-minute fuss might be: a simple colourful hors d'oeuvre of artichoke hearts or avocados, mozzarella and tomatoes sprinkled with fresh basil leaves and vinaigrette; a leg of Welsh lamb with honey, garlic and rosemary (I learned the recipe from a regular weekend guest) served with thinly layered potatoes baked in milk (roast potatoes need too much attention), and a fresh vegetable. Pudding is ready in advance: baby meringues baked overnight in the Rayburn's warming drawer during the week, and individual lemon or lime syllabubs, made on Friday.

One of the least exacting, but still proper, Sunday lunches is a roast chicken baked in a terracotta brick. Cooked this way the timing is not critical and the chicken always turns out tender and juicy. I add lemon, butter and fresh thyme to produce a light sauce which tastes delicious with baked potatoes, baked parsnips and a watercress salad. Pudding depends on appetites: blackberries and apples can either be turned into a creamy fool, or a more substantial crumble.

As teatime marks the end of most weekends, it seems to warrant a final indulgence, especially after a hearty walk. My fruitcake-making is still at the novice stage, and sponges need to be eaten fresh from the oven, so I stick to flapjacks and brownies which keep well, and can be made before the weekend.

Sausage puff pie

Steak, kidney and mushroom casserole (serves 4)

750g (1½lb) chuck steak, cubed
8 lambs kidneys, skinned and chopped
250g (½lb) mushrooms
2 onions, finely chopped
1 can Guinness
2 tablespoons Worcester sauce
salt, black pepper
home-made bouquet garni of fresh thyme, parsley & rosemary
60g (2oz) butter

Fry the onions until soft, then remove with a slatted spoon to a large casserole. Add more butter to the frying pan and brown the steak, then the kidney pieces, transferring each batch to the casserole. Pour in the Guinness and Worcester sauce, and add the bouquet garni, salt and pepper. Leave in a moderate oven 325°F/160°C, gas mark 3 for 3 to 4 hours. About 30 minutes before serving, lightly fry the mushrooms and add to the meat. This tastes even better if made the day before and reheated.

Sausage puff pie (serves 4/5)

430g (14oz) puff pastry
370g (¾lb) pork sausage meat
1 finely chopped onion
2 eggs
2 fresh sage leaves
sea salt
black pepper

Choose a rectangular baking dish, then roll out the pastry into an oblong twice the size. Mix together the sausage meat, onion, one egg, salt and pepper and minutely chopped sage leaves. Fit the pastry into the dish, leaving an overlap on all sides, and spread the sausage mixture evenly inside. Seal the pastry edges together along the top, then glaze all over with a beaten egg. Bake at a high heat (400°F/200°C, gas mark 6) for 1 hour.

Serve hot, warm or cold with a hot tomato sauce.

Lime syllabub (serves 6)

Juice and grated rind of 1 large lime (or 2 lemons if lime is not available)
90g (3oz) icing sugar
1 glass of dry sherry or white wine
600ml (1pt) double cream, whipped

Soak the lime rind in the juice and sherry or wine, plus the sugar, for at least four hours, or overnight if possible. Transfer the mixture into a large bowl and gradually add the stiffly whipped cream, stirring gently until well blended. Spoon the syllabub into glasses and keep chilled.

Nicola Cox

A Travelling Gourmet

My kitchen is at the centre of my house, so it's the heart (or, perhaps more accurately, the stomach) of the house. It's the focal point, the inevitable crossroads for the goings out and the comings in, frequently with muddy boots or paws. It's a warm place in which the family and other animals congregate naturally, but I'm not averse to escaping from it, in spite of its wonderful view, during the golden days of summer. It's well-equipped and efficient as well as being a comfortable friendly room, packed with treasures brought back from abroad, like my lovely Portuguese duck soup tureen from the Oporto fairground which sits on the pine-dresser with plates from Alsace and pots from Cyprus. It's got Granny's old pine kitchen table, which seemed so huge when I sat at it as a child, and the old black hooks still hang from the ceiling, so useful for sausages and for drying herbs for the cupboard and flowers for my *pot pourri*.

It's a room to live in, entertain in, and cook in, and it's the room in which I give my cookery demonstrations; hence it is the scene of some of my triumphs and the odd disaster! Having tested and tried out a new dish on the family, it is a wonderful moment when it is hailed as a delicious success by twenty-five discriminating people. On the other hand one never forgets those horrific moments when disaster strikes. One day in particular, with three chefs in the back row watching to see if they wanted me to join their demonstration team, is forever engraved on my memory. The bottom fell out of the liquidiser when it was full of an incredibly complicated sauce, and not only did I have to start making it again but I was left skating on a

lethal pond. And I still shudder whenever I see the scar on my finger and remember how the cleaver nearly took it off instead of splitting the pig's trotter, and how I tried to keep going in spite of what seemed like an unstaunchable flow of blood!

But although cooking, thinking, talking and writing about food is my career, it is still a pleasure and joy to me, particularly if I can do it for friends in my own kitchen. I think the food we cook reflects our personality, and, being half-Scots, I rarely use extravagant ingredients, although I absolutely insist on freshness and quality and try to use what is good at the time. In the country kitchen, the garden and seasons are never far away, and the first trip of the year round the garden for a salad is an important day; over-wintered lettuce, lamb's lettuce; stonecrop (a weed which tastes like watercress), a little early sorrel and salad burnet and perhaps some Italian chicory, the common dandelion (covered with a flowerpot to blanch it) and some pallid-looking endive from the cellar. Dress up this *mesclun* with best olive or walnut oil, chopped chervil (which is always up early) and perhaps a home-made mint or basil wine vinegar, and you have a treat reminiscent of the best summer days. Years of moving round the world with the Army have made me really appreciate my herb garden, now laid out with fifty or more culinary, medicinal and scented herbs.

Entertaining seems to fit the kitchen and, whatever the occasion, I like to cook as creatively as possible. For simplicity, what could look or taste better or be easier than my big round Strasbourg plate with circles of crisp yellow courgette alternating with rosy salami (from my ceiling hooks), with little yellow and red tomatoes from the greenhouse and big blue-black Kalamati olives? Or the stunning colours of an orange salad in syrup, flavoured with orange-flower water and decorated with tiny sprigs of peppermint geranium from the windowsill? But I also love to find time to cook special dishes, and I am including here the recipe, Crown Diana, which I created for the Royal Wedding in 1981. This is a coronet of meringue holding a scoop of honey ice cream and robed in a royal purple sauce of blackcurrant, raspberry and liqueur de cassis. It tastes as good as it looks. I am also including a lovely new recipe, Stuffed Chicken Breasts in Summer Sauce, to show how well the *nouvelle cuisine* translates into the English countryside.

I am happy so long as both kitchen and company contrive to create an atmosphere in which I can entertain and invent all the year round.

Stuffed chicken breasts in summer sauce
(serves 4)

Nearly all my cooking is designed for the cook hostess so that she can enjoy her own entertaining; this dish is ideal as it can be served hot or cold, with all the hard work done beforehand.

4 suprêmes of chicken (breasts only)
30g (1oz) butter
1 tablespoon chopped parsley
a little fresh chopped or pinch of dried tarragon
a little grated lemon rind
a tiny bit of garlic
½ lemon with which to rub suprêmes
salt and pepper

Sauce
3 tablespoons olive oil
1 small finely chopped shallot, spring onion or little bit of onion
1 small finely chopped carrot
½ clove garlic
¼ bay leaf
sprig lemon thyme or thyme
2–3 parsley stalks

sprig fresh or pinch of dried tarragon
2 tablespoons dry white vermouth
150ml (¼pt) dry white wine
150ml (¼pt) chicken stock and ¼ stock cube (Knorr)
225ml (8fl oz) double cream
fresh chives, tarragon and chervil, or just parsley
salt and pepper

Sauce
Gently heat the oil in a wide sauté pan or frying pan with lid; add the shallot and carrot and cook gently until softened but not browned; add the chopped garlic, bay leaf, herbs, vermouth and wine, and simmer half-covered for 15 minutes until well reduced; add the stock and cube and reduce again, uncovered, until only about 150ml (¼pt) of syrupy liquid remains. Now add the cream to the pan and season lightly; simmer and reduce again until of a nice coating sauce consistency. Strain the sauce through a fine sieve, preferably lined with muslin, and squeeze and press out all the sauce from the vegetables and herbs which you discard. Keep the sauce a little thicker than you want it, to allow for it to thin a little with the juices from the chicken breasts. Return the sauce to a lidded pan, wide enough to take the chicken breasts in one layer.

Suprêmes
Prepare the suprêmes by removing the skin and the tendon in the breast fillet. Cream the butter, herbs, lemon, garlic and seasoning together, and form into four rolls. Cut a little pocket by inserting a knife longways into the thick part of the breast. Slip in a roll of herb butter and pinch the edges of the slit together again. Rub with a little lemon juice and season lightly.

Add the prepared suprêmes to the sauce, cover and poach very gently, the sauce barely bubbling, turning once, for about 10–14 minutes until they feel just resilient to the touch all through. Add the chives, scissored in 1cm (½-inch) lengths and the very roughly chopped tarragon and chervil (or whatever herbs you have) to the sauce just before the end of the cooking, adding enough to give flavour and a pretty green speckled sauce; correct seasoning. Serve at once (though it will keep warm) or leave to cool, covered, and serve cold. The sauce stays creamy and flowing.

Parigino (serves 6–8 people)

I often pick up ideas whilst travelling abroad; I saw this in Piedmont in one of those gloriously displayed windows of food. It's so pretty and perfect for summer buffet parties.

500g (1lb) thinly sliced ham
½ diced green pepper
1 diced red pepper
1 diced pickled dill cucumber
120g (4oz) cooked peas or beans
120g (4oz) cooked diced carrot
120g (4oz) peeled, seeded and diced tomatoes
1–2 tablespoons pistachio nuts
600ml (1pt) packet aspic jelly crystals
1 tablespoon marsala
2 teaspoons tarragon vinegar
a little chopped fresh tarragon (if available)

Blanch the peppers in boiling salt water for 30 seconds, then refresh with cold water to set the colour. Cook peas and carrots and refresh them also to set the colour. Make up the aspic jelly with 300ml (½pt) water, stir in the marsala and vinegar and make up to 600ml (1pt) with cold water. Leave until cold and syrupy. Line a deep, long, 1.2 litre (2pt) terrine with ham slices; then fill with layers of diced mixed vegetables, pistachio nuts, tarragon and seasoning between layers of ham. Press down lightly. Pour in the aspic to seep between the layers and to hold it all together. Leave until set. Turn out and serve in slices.

Old-fashioned stuffed shoulder of lamb
(adapted from Hannah Glasse) (serves 6–8)

Oysters were used in this, but I have adapted it to the more available prawn. Anchovy is added to the sauce: this gives a really rich and tasty dish, great for the winter months.

2kg (4lb) (or so) shoulder of lamb

Stuffing
60g (2oz) breadcrumbs
3 hard-boiled eggs
120g (4oz) prawns or oysters
30g (1oz) beef suet
3 anchovy fillets
1 finely chopped onion
1 teaspoon fresh chopped or good pinch dried thyme
1 teaspoon chopped winter or summer savory or parsley
1 egg
1 teaspoon oyster or anchovy sauce (optional)
salt, pepper and nutmeg

Sauce
2 tablespoons finely chopped onion
15g (½oz) butter
15g (½oz) plain flour
100ml (4fl oz) red wine

225ml (8fl oz) stock, vegetable water or stock cube and water
1 teaspoon oyster or anchovy sauce
1–2 anchovies
salt, pepper and nutmeg

Bone out the shoulder of lamb, stuff and sew up. Tie once or twice and roast in a moderately hot oven (190°C/375°F, gas mark 5) for about 2 hours, basting from time to time. Remove to a serving dish, de-grease the roasting pan, add the prepared sauce and stir in all brown, tasty roasting juices. Serve with roast.

Stuffing
Chop the hard-boiled eggs with the anchovy, prawns or oysters and beef suet, add in the breadcrumbs, onion, herbs, oyster or anchovy sauce, if used, and seasoning. Bind with the egg and use to stuff the shoulder of lamb.

Sauce
Gently fry the finely chopped onion in the butter until soft, add the flour and cook for several minutes; then draw off the stove, wait for the sizzling to cease before adding wine, stock, oyster or anchovy sauce, chopped anchovies and seasoning. Bring to the boil, whisking, and simmer for 5–10 minutes before using.

Melted butter sauce (for 750g (1½lb) vegetables)

Here is another Old English recipe which seems to have slipped out of favour, heaven knows why, for it is the simplest thing in the world and ideal for dressing up baby vegetables, like carrots, beans or courgettes.

½ teaspoon flour
60g (2oz) butter
2 tablespoons milk
salt and pepper
very finely chopped parsley

Mix the butter and flour together and put in a saucepan with the milk. Heat until boiling, shaking the pan all the time until a creamy sauce forms. Add the hot well-drained cooked vegetables, seasoning and chopped parsley, and shake to coat the vegetables with the sauce, which is really just a glaze.

Crown Diana (serves 4–6)

I like producing dishes for special occasions. Jubilee Seafood Starter, evolved in 1977, is now a firm favourite and I'm already very fond of this dish, created to celebrate the Royal Wedding of 1981.

Meringue
3 egg whites
180g (6oz) castor sugar

Honey ice cream
3 egg yolks
300ml (½pt) milk
150ml (¼pt) double cream
150g (5oz) honey

Sauce
120g (4oz) raspberries
120g (4oz) blackcurrants
60g (2oz) sugar
2–3 tablespoons liqueur de cassis
100ml (4fl oz) water

Meringue
Whisk the egg whites until just holding a peak; then whisk in about 2 tablespoons of sugar and continue whisking until very stiff and shiny before folding in the remaining sugar. Mark 9cm (3½-inch) diameter circles on a piece of bakewell paper. Turn the meringue into a piping bag with a large nozzle, and carefully pipe a thin layer round and round to fill in the circle. Pipe another layer round the outside to make a raised wall, then top this with blobs drawn up to peaks, so that it looks like a crown. Bake in a slow oven (110°C/225°F, gas mark ¼) until pale golden and completely crisp. Cool on a rack and keep in an airtight tin.

Honey ice cream
Heat the honey and milk but do not boil or it may curdle. Whisk the yolks briefly and gradually pour on the hot milk and honey. Return to a heavy pan and cook over a low heat or use a double boiler (though not aluminium, which discolours egg-yolk mixtures) or bowl over hot water. Heat gently, stirring until the custard thickens a little and coats the back of the spoon, but do *not* boil or the yolks will curdle. Cool, add the cream, chill and freeze, stirring sides to the middle with a fork as it freezes; once firm, process in a food processor or whisk until smooth. Re-freeze until required. Mellow in fridge before using.

Sauce
Cook the blackcurrants with the sugar and water until tender; cool, drain and purée with the raspberries, adding enough of the reserved juice to make a coating sauce. Sieve, add in the cassis to taste, and chill.

To assemble
Set a scoop of honey ice cream in the meringue crown and coat with royal purple sauce. Serve at once.

Shona Crawford Poole

Puddings and Pies

My favourite wooden spoon comes from Zambia. It has a slender tapered handle and a generous bowl and it feels right in the hand. My saucepans are Swiss, the coffee cups are French, and the stacking steamer baskets were bought warm from the lap of the man who made them in the Hong Kong street where the daily jade market takes place. Beside them is a cartwheel of a Brie basket which swanks a whole cheese for parties and doubles as a tray on normal duties. It came home from the south of France in a glider trailer together with the inevitable string of garlic and cheeses which caused the eyes of the customs man to water by the time they landed at Dover.

The beautiful old preserving pan, its brass shining through a century of bumps and service, was a bargain bought by torchlight in Brick Lane, a small-hours-of-Saturday-night-and-Sunday-morning market in London's East End. It is English all right, which is more than can be said of most of the 'things' in my kitchen and much of what is cooked in it. And yet, in a way, the dishes that come out of it are very typical of the food that any enthusiastic cook will be making today.

I attempt the most enjoyable of the dishes I have eaten in restaurants, or read about in books or the colour supplements. I try to recreate the tastes of other people's cooking – my grandmothers', mother's, friends'. Writing about food is a licence to be nosey about it, to question chefs and colleagues, and sometimes to dip a finger in their pots and pans. Travel provides inspiration at every turn, and with a job that encompasses both subjects I often find myself bombarded by more stimulus than I can cope with and too little time to try out half the ideas it would be interesting to work on.

It is probably just because I do lead such a modern metropolitan life – eating in foreign restaurants and cooking dishes from anywhere and everywhere – that traditional English pies have a special place in my affections and in my repertoire. The very act of making them evokes pictures of a more gracious and more leisured age.

Savoury puddings and mighty pies are the stuff of hunt breakfasts and harvest suppers, of gentlemen's clubs and flagstoned farmhouse kitchens. Yet these most distinctively English of dishes are at risk of becoming endangered species. Their once fine reputation is well on the way to being ruined by pub grub, and their substantial nutritional value is as out of fashion as John Bull's figure.

If anything gives us reason to regret the passing of an age when girth was a sign of wealth it is the incomparable aroma of a good steak and kidney pudding when its suet crust is breached. And I wonder how many people have tasted a pudding made with partridge, grouse or pheasant. Less elegant than a roasted bird perhaps, but all the flavour of the game is captured in its own strong gravy, and there are no bones to fight round the plate.

Suet puddings filled with meat and boiled in a basin do not seem to have appeared in cookery books until the late seventeenth century, though by the nineteenth century they had become an indispensable feature of the national diet. Pies go back much further. Take a fourteenth-century recipe for *tartes of flesh* that appears in a collection made by the master cooks of King Richard II. It calls for small birds, joints of young rabbit, and a forcemeat of cooked pork, hard-boiled eggs and cheese seasoned with spices, salt, sugar and saffron. All this was baked in a standing *coffyn* of pastry.

Spicing and sweetening meat and fish are no longer the rule. But modern mince pies, which are still sometimes made with meat, and invariably with mincemeat containing suet, follow that strand of our pie heritage. Medieval principles of construction live on in the raised pies made today.

Coffyns of pastry are still being raised, and often by hand too, for game pies, veal-and-ham pies, and for the famous pork pies of Melton Mowbray. None of the very old recipes I have found is very specific about the pastry, just as recipes for bread are largely absent from early cookery books. Their authors seem to have assumed that these were skills one learned at one's mother's elbow.

The pastry of the mighty pies of old was not always intended to be eaten. For Yorkshire's giant Christmas pies made with boned birds of increasing size wrapped, Russian-doll fashion, one round another, the thick pastry walls were a protective shell and carrying case for cooked delicacies sealed in butter to preserve them. So perhaps the choice of pastry was left to the cook's discretion and depended on the size and purpose of the pie.

Puddings and Pies 53

Traditional English pies

Today, the pastry is expected to be not just edible, but crisp and full of flavour, and modern recipes have pretty standard proportions of flour, fat and liquid. It takes courage and a little practice to mould a free-standing *coffyn* by hand from a ball of dough. The alternative is to use a metal mould with a base and separate side-pieces held in place with clips. Both the traditional pointed-oval game-pie shape and straight-sided rectangular pie moulds have patterned walls which give home-made pies a pleasingly professional-looking finish.

It was a game pie from Fortnum and Mason that stimulated my first efforts to bake these classic pies. I had been reading recipes for them for years before I took the plunge, and the results were so rewarding that I have been making them ever since.

Freshly baked pies freeze very well and are an invaluable standby for impromptu entertaining or for distributing the work for a party over several days. I usually make two at a time so that there is one for now and one for later.

Success with pies led to experiments with puddings and these are equally obliging. Once cooked they can be refrigerated for a day or two, or frozen, and reheated with no ill-effects. Frozen puddings should be thawed completely before reheating for at least an hour before serving.

Game pie (serves 6 to 8)

Filling
450g (1lb) venison, hare, pheasant, grouse or partridge (meat only)
120ml (4fl oz) port
Freshly ground black pepper
450g (1lb) pork, lean and fat
110g (4oz) smoked bacon, lean and fat
1 medium onion
1 teaspoon finely chopped fresh sage
2 tablespoons finely chopped fresh parsley
1 teaspoon finely grated lemon zest
225g (8oz) fresh pork sausage meat

Jellied stock
900g (2lb) veal bones and game carcases
1 medium onion
1 carrot
2 bay leaves

Pastry
450g (1lb) plain flour, or 500g (1lb 2oz) 81% wholemeal flour
1 teaspoon salt
85g (3oz) lard
250ml (8fl oz) water
1 egg yolk beaten with 1 tablespoon water, to glaze

Filling
Cut the meat off the game and reserve the carcases for stock. Slice the meat into strips about 5cm (2 inches) long by about 7mm (¼ inch) wide and thick. Reserve the trimmings and marinate the strips in the port with a little pepper.

Put the game trimmings, pork, bacon and peeled onion through the coarse blade of a mincer, or chop them finely. Add the herbs and lemon zest and season the mixture generously with salt and pepper. Mix well together.

Form teaspoonfuls of the sausagemeat into balls, rolling them in the palms of your hands, and set these aside too.

Stock
Put the bones and carcases in a large pot and add the roughly chopped vegetables. Cover with cold water and bring to the boil. Skim thoroughly before adding the bay leaves, a little salt and plenty of freshly ground pepper. Simmer the stock for about two hours then strain it through a sieve lined with a double thickness of butter muslin or cheesecloth. Reduce the stock by fast boiling to about 300ml (½pt) and set it aside.

Pastry
Sift the flour and salt into a warmed mixing bowl. Put the butter, lard and water into a small saucepan and heat until the fat has melted. Bring to the boil and pour the mixture immediately into the flour, stirring vigorously with a wooden spoon to make a pliable dough. Continue stirring until the dough is cool enough to handle. Turn it on to a lightly floured board and knead it until it is

smooth. Rest the dough, covered, in a warm place for about 30 minutes.

To assemble the pie
Lightly grease an oval or rectangular pie mould of about 1.5 litres (2½pt) capacity, or use a loose-bottomed 18cm (7-inch) round cake tin.

Roll out about two-thirds of the pastry to line the mould. Fold the pastry in half and lower it carefully into the tin. Unfold it and ease it smoothly across the base and up the sides of the mould. Press the pastry well into the join between the base and sides of the mould and into any fancy indentations on its sides. The pastry lining should be no less than 7mm (¼ inch) thick. If it is thinner the pie crust may split, and if it is much thicker there will too much soggy dough between the meat and the crust.

Put half the minced pork and bacon mixture in the bottom of the tin. Drain and pat dry the slivers of marinated game and lay the strips lengthwise on top of the pork, interspersing them with balls of sausagemeat. Cover with the remaining pork and bacon, pressing the pie filling lightly into the tin and shaping the mixture into a shallow dome.

Roll the remaining pastry to a thickness of about 7mm (¼ inch). Moisten the edges. Lift it on the rolling pin and lay it over the pie. Press the lid on firmly and trim the pastry with a sharp knife. To decorate the edge and ensure a good seal, press round the crust with the back of a fork. Cut a 2.5cm (1-inch) cross through the pastry in the centre of the lid, and fold back the four points to make a good opening for escaping steam. Re-roll the trimmings and cut decorative leaves and flowers. Stick them on to the pie with beaten egg glaze, then paint all the exposed pastry with egg.

Stand the pie on a baking sheet and bake it in a preheated hot oven (230°C/450°F, gas mark 8) for 20 minutes, then reduce the heat to moderate (160°C/325°F, gas mark 3), cover the pie loosely with foil, and bake it for another 3 hours. Remove the foil for the last 30 minutes of cooking time. Leave the pie in its mould until it is almost cold.

When the pie is nearly cold remove the mould and pour into it as much of the cool, liquid stock as it will accept. Pour it in slowly through a small funnel or icing nozzle. Leave the pie in a cool place for several hours before serving. The stock will set to a jelly, filling the gaps between the pastry and the meat which will have shrunk during cooking. Serve the pie cold, cut into slices or wedges.

To make a traditional pork pie of similar size to the game pie, use the same pastry recipe and method. Chop finely about 1kg (2lb) or a little more pork. The meat should have a good proportion of fat if the pie is not to be dry. Season it generously with freshly ground black pepper, and a little salt and finely chopped fresh sage. To make the jellied stock boil veal and pork bones with a couple of onions, and parsley, thyme, sage and bay. Bake as for the game pie.

Game puddings are an ideal way of cooking birds of uncertain age since the long, slow steaming is almost certain to ensure that the flesh will be tender. This recipe works equally well with grouse and partridge, or a mixture of birds.

Pheasant pudding (serves 4)

Filling
1 large pheasant weighing about 1.2kg (2½lb)
1 onion, quartered
4 juniper berries, crushed
1 bouquet garni of parsley, thyme, celery and bay leaves
salt and freshly ground black pepper

Crust
225g (8oz) self-raising flour
110g (4oz) shredded beef suet
water to mix

Cut the breast meat off the pheasant and divide each piece into large, bite-sized chunks. Cut off as much of the meat remaining on the bird as can be removed easily, and set all the flesh aside.

Break up the carcase and put it in a pan with the onion, juniper berries and bouquet garni. Add 900ml (1½pt) water and a little salt and pepper and bring to the boil. Skim, then simmer the stock, uncovered, for about 1½ hours. Strain the stock, which should measure about 300ml (½pt).

To make the crust, sift the flour and salt into a bowl and add the suet. Mix lightly together with a fork. Sprinkle the mixture with cold water, and mix lightly, adding more water as necessary until the dough holds together. Using your hands, gather it into a ball and knead it lightly.

On a floured surface, roll out the dough to a circle which will cover an upturned pudding basin of about 1.5 litres (2½pt) capacity. Cut a wedge from the circle (about a quarter of the total area), and re-roll this piece for the lid. Use the remaining dough to line the basin, dampening the edges to be joined.

Toss the pheasant meat in well-seasoned flour and pack it into the basin. Pour in stock to come about two-thirds of the way up the filling. Fold the dough lining which is proud of the edge of the basin over the filling and dampen the edge. Top with the lid and press lightly to seal.

Cover the bowl with buttered greaseproof paper and foil which have been folded together to make a 2.5cm (1-inch) pleat across the diameter of the basin. Tie the covering down firmly with string.

Stand the pudding in a large saucepan and pour in boiling water to come half-way up the sides of the basin. Bring back to the boil and simmer, covered, for about three hours, being careful that the water does not go off the boil or the saucepan boil dry. Add boiling water, as necessary, to bring up the level.

Serve the pudding in its basin with a clean white cloth pinned round it. Just before serving, cut a small round hole in the crust and pour in a little more hot stock.

Steak and kidney pudding has many variations. Some recipes call for stewing beef, others for rump steak. Sometimes the meat is cubed, while other recipes suggest beating strips flat and rolling a piece of kidney in the middle. One recipe calls for onion, another for none. But the great Escoffier certainly had the right idea when he said that 'there is nothing more simple and yet more difficult for those without experience than the making of English steak pies, puddings and their derivatives. The reason for this is that once the dish has been made up and cooked there is very little that can be done to correct any mistakes made with the seasoning, the quantity of liquid used, or the cooking time.'

Here is my steak and kidney pudding. My butcher thinks I am mad to use rump, and tuts at what he sees as extravagance. But then he belongs to the cook-the-meat-first school of pudding makers, and we agree to differ.

Steak and kidney pudding (serves 4)

Filling
570g (1¼lb) rump steak
110g (4oz) ox kidney
4 tablespoons well-seasoned flour
300ml (½pt) good beef stock

Crust
225g (8oz) self-raising flour
1 teaspoon salt
110g (4oz) shredded beef suet
water to mix

Remove all skin and fat from the steak and cut it into strips about 2.5cm (1 inch) wide and 7.5cm (3 inches) long. Core the kidney and cut it into small bite-sized pieces. Flatten the strips of beef by beating them with a rolling pin, then dip each piece in seasoned flour and roll it up round a piece of kidney.

Make the crust, fill and cook the pudding using the directions given in the previous recipe.

Tamasin Day-Lewis

A Game Feast

When I left home, my culinary future didn't look at all promising. The only things I could cook from memory were bacon and eggs and spaghetti bolognese. I don't blame my school, which did its best to teach us the basics; I blame my greed. I would cook the statutory madeira cake, meringues or Esse biscuits as fast as I could – half the mixture always got eaten raw – and spend the rest of the lesson devising ways of making my creation as unappetising as possible. Inky blue meringues and livid green cake didn't seem to appeal to the rest of the dormitory! My greed finally got the better of me, and I started avidly watching and skivvying for all the good cooks I knew, and committing to memory and paper their techniques and recipes. Gradually it began to dawn on me why a lot of good cooks positively enjoy slaving over a hot stove.

My first kitchen was bright red, very tall and about five feet square, rather like being inside a pillar-box, but I managed to hold a Christmas party for 25 three years running, with the food getting more ambitious each time. Finished dishes had to be stored next door in the bath, syllabubs shrinking shyly from a marinading saddle of venison.

By the time I went to Cambridge I was already a committed cook, and used to constraints of space, so I confronted the 'gyp room' with something approaching equanimity. It featured a nursery-sized Baby Belling, a temperamental gas-ring, and a fridge that was periodically and indiscriminately raided by ravenous colleagues. I quickly discovered that the best way of commandeering these facilities and ensuring reasonable standards was to cook for everyone on my staircase. Consequently there were dinner-parties every night where we ate something huge and filling that could be made in one pot. We were undoubtedly and self-consciously budding gourmets, sampling squid stewed in its own ink with white wine, tomatoes and garlic; a casserole of belly pork simmered in marsala; slow-braised pigs' liver on a bed of cubed root vegetables; a wholewheat lasagne with chicken livers or spinach and ricotta.

I graduated to summer holidays in the West of Ireland, where friends and I tried to buy as little as possible. My host, Alec Wallace, when not studying Elizabethan cypher or the history of mathematical notation, built his house, fished and planted a vegetable garden overflowing with exotica which that corner of Mayo had probably never seen. Local shops usually stopped at cabbage and carrots. Alec's garden was resplendent with everything from Florentine fennel to aubergines, and included a dead oak tree that yielded a wonderful crop of delicate oyster mushrooms.

The kitchen became a culinary laboratory, filled with bloated guinea-pigs. In the morning we made spinach or carageen soda bread, and most afternoons we tended the lobster pots and caught mackerel, which we either rolled in oatmeal and ate grilled, or sold on the quay at Old Head for a penny each.

In the evening, Alec recreated food from his travels through Turkey, Iran and Afghanistan; a bulgur salad of plumped cracked wheat with finely chopped onion, mint and tomato and full medames, or cabbage leaves wrapped dolmades-style around spiced minced lamb and baked in stock.

After working in a series of ill-equipped kitchens as a professional cook, and living with a further series of ill-designed ones in Norfolk, I finally came to planning my own in Somerset. It was built by a remarkable carpenter who was about to abandon his trade for a career in political economy. He scoured the Bristol wood-yards for best Brazilian mahogany and Columbian pine for work-surfaces and cupboards; sunk a beautiful pink slab of marble into one work-top, and built a corner cupboard and vegetable rack with leftover bits. My one rough sketch was carried out to the letter, including a fitted dresser on one wall copied from drawings in an Elizabethan kitchen book.

Cooking has become even more of a test of the imagination without the sort of shops that sell things like fresh pasta, calves' liver and sweetbreads, but gradually local discoveries have made up for it. Chanterelles can be found in the beech woods in the autumn, and tossed with olive oil into a nutty buckwheat spaghetti. Whortleberries from the Quantocks are delicious in sorbets, tarts or jam. A local fish-shop has monkfish, which we cook on the barbecue en brochette, and wings of skate, which are delicious poached and served 'in the grass' on a bed of watercress or sorrel purée.

Corn-fed capons, ducks and Christmas geese come from a nearby farm, and game from a rather unusual source, a local pub which shall remain nameless. I never know what I'll come home with, but could probably go all winter without seeing my butcher. Pheasant, partridge, woodcock, wild duck, hare, rabbit and venison are priced and bagged over a drink and taken home. There is one slight snag: we have to do the plucking, skinning and gutting ourselves.

A Game Feast 59

Tamasin Day-Lewis

Still life with marinade

I'll never forget our first attempt with a brace of pheasants. I sat outside on the mounting block with my husband (who is allergic to feathers), a giant bin-liner and Mrs Beeton's trusty instructions, getting spattered with blood. The tail feathers wouldn't budge, and by the time we'd finished, the birds looked as though they'd been mugged and we were swearing we'd become vegetarians. Since then we've improved, and I enjoy cooking game more than anything.

Depending on the age and quality of the meat, it can be cooked by either the quick-fast or the long-slow method. Sometimes I roast until rare, basting with a herb butter as often as I remember. I marry bird and sauce or gravy at the last minute, and usually use fruit in either the stuffing or the sauce. Strongly flavoured game is, surprisingly, greatly enhanced by other strong tastes. Pigeon can be coated with a rich juniper sauce, wild duck stuffed with wild apricots and hazelnuts or prunes and brown rice, and saddle of venison roasted and served with tart crab-apple jelly or damson sauce.

If I am slow-cooking, I'll casserole a haunch of venison with a port and elderberry sauce, stew rabbit with green ginger, mustard and mushrooms, or hare with a sweet and sour combination of glazed shallots and an aïllade.

Now that I've got plenty of space both indoors and out, I can no longer use the kitchen as an excuse for failure. (I use my baby Miranda instead!) But this doesn't stop each meal being at once an agony and a delight, both relaxation and competition, not with anyone in particular, but with the shimmering mirage of perfection that hangs tantalisingly over every pot and pan.

Wild rabbit smothered in mustard and green ginger (serves 4)

1 wild rabbit, jointed
600ml (1pt) good stock
150ml (¼pt) dry white wine
3 or 4 sprigs of thyme
250g (8oz) mushrooms
1 tablespoon strong mustard powder (English)
1 tablespoon moutarde de Meaux
1 tablespoon green ginger put through garlic crusher
1 large onion
4 cloves garlic
olive oil
flour
salt and pepper

In a deep casserole sweat the onion and garlic in olive oil until translucent and soft. Transfer to a plate. Roll the rabbit in seasoned flour and brown it in the oil. Return the onion and garlic to the casserole.

Add the wine, stock, seasoning and herbs, and simmer in a low oven 120°C/250°–275°F, gas mark ½–1) until tender. Add the lightly fried mushrooms, kept whole if small, about 30 minutes before the end of cooking time.

Transfer the rabbit joints and mushrooms to a plate and keep hot. Reduce the sauce, adding the mustards and green ginger at the last minute, and stirring well. Return the rabbit and mushrooms to the casserole, and serve.

Prune and rice stuffing

This is a delicious stuffing for wild duck, pheasant or partridge, also for a boned leg of lamb.

180g (6oz) brown rice
120g (4oz) prunes, soaked, cooked and chopped
2 tablespoons blanched, split almonds
½ teaspoon coriander
1 Cox's orange pippin, chopped or grated
1 egg, well beaten
salt
pepper

Cook the rice in the normal way, and mix it with the remaining ingredients. Stuff the birds or joint, and roast.

Sweet and sour casserole of hare (serves 6)

If possible, use only the saddle, otherwise the saddle and back legs only.

6 jointed pieces of hare
red wine almost to cover
250g (8oz) mushrooms
3 bay leaves
4 sprigs of thyme
flour
salt
pepper
olive oil

Roll the pieces of hare in the seasoned flour, and fry on both sides in olive oil for about 2 minutes a side, in a large casserole. Gradually add the wine, then the herbs, and bring to a very gentle simmer. Continue cooking for 1½ hours or until tender. Add the mushrooms fried lightly in olive oil at the end of the cooking.

Aïllade (sour)
1 medium onion
12 crushed juniper berries
liver and blood of the hare
1 glass red wine
1 glass red wine vinegar
3 cloves of garlic

Chop finely as for a duxelles the onion, liver and garlic, add the other ingredients, and simmer at a mere bubble for 1½ hours. Add to the casserole.

Glazed shallots (sweet)
24 shallots
30g (1oz) butter
2 teaspoons brown sugar

Cook the shallots in boiling water for about 5 minutes or until just not resistant to a knife point. Then glaze them in the sugar and butter until soft, and add to the casserole.

It is delicious served with potato and celeriac croquettes.

Potato and celeriac croquettes (serves 6)

3 large potatoes
milk
butter
1 medium celeriac
1 egg
salt
pepper
nutmeg
olive oil

Cook and mash the potatoes with milk and butter. Peel and cut the celeriac into matchstick strips, and blanch for a couple of minutes in boiling water. Add to the potato with a well-beaten egg, and mix thoroughly. Season. Leave to cool, when the croquettes are easier to mould. This is easiest if done with a tablespoon. Fry in olive oil until crisp.

Saddle of venison with a port and elderberry sauce (serves 8)

2kg (4lb) venison
500g (1lb) mushrooms
6 cloves garlic
1 large onion
olive oil
flour

Marinade
1 bottle of decent red wine
12 crushed juniper berries
1 large onion (sliced)
2 tablespoons red wine vinegar
2 tablespoons brandy
6 bay leaves
pepper and salt

Sauce
(I use my homemade elderberry and apple jelly, but any tart jelly would do.)
250g (8oz) elderberry jelly
1 tablespoon brown sugar
¼ bottle of port
peeled rind of 1 lemon
pinch of cinnamon

Cut the venison into large chunks, about 5cm (2 inches) square. Cover with the marinade ingredients for anything from two to six days, turning when you remember.

On the day, slice the garlic, mushrooms and onion, and brown in olive oil in a heavy casserole. Add the venison to the browning vegetables, and sprinkle with flour, turning to cover evenly. Brown for 5 minutes. Add the strained marinade, cover and simmer gently for 2 hours or until tender. Ten minutes before serving put the sauce ingredients in a pan and boil hard until thick, syrupy and reduced. Remove the peel, and add the sauce to the casserole at the last moment, before serving.

Delicious with *pommes Dauphinoise* and a parsnip or swede and carrot purée.

Lady Camilla Dempster

Infidelity in the Kitchen

This time it will be different. This time while Nigel is away I shall go to bed early after a light supper of cheese and water-biscuits, and when he comes back I shall be thinner.

It never is different. That sort of domestic behaviour lasts for one evening and then I revert to indulgence and extravagance in the kitchen. It is not that I don't like cheese and water-biscuits. It is just that I prefer them to end a meal rather than form the whole of it.

Although my husband was born in Calcutta and describes himself as a colonial, he shows all the traits of a suspicious Englishman when it comes to food. He shuns the idea of eating any animal whose origins are not immediately apparent. Lamb and beef and pork must be instantly recognisable, and fish has to be accompanied by chips and come from a takeaway. Garlic is only tolerated, pasta is regarded as restaurant food, and if he does eat anything with a sauce around it, it is only as a vehicle for mashed potato.

These strictures mean that while the preparation of the food is simple enough, the cooking of it is hardly challenging. The recipes which appear here are not complicated, but they all contain one or more ingredients from which he would recoil. So, after he has gone, the garlic press, the pasta machine and the fish kettle are taken out of the cupboard, and I telephone a greedy friend. Sometimes we are defeated by our ideas and I have to seek professional advice, as on the occasion when I bought a whole turbot from a mobile fishmonger. My most greedy friend had been asked to lunch, but as the afternoon wore on it became increasingly clear that neither of us was capable of cooking it. The fish was looking particularly dismal on a white china dish. Finally I telephoned the chef of Le Suquet, and he, mollified by the fluency of my French, described how it should be decapitated, definned and cooked in a court-bouillon until the flesh just came away from the bone. We ate it at four o'clock with Hollandaise sauce and new potatoes and it tasted marvellous.

Ideally, the girlfriends in question should be thin and single. If married, they usually have to be at home cooking dinner for their husbands; and if they are not thin, they tend to feel they should be, and don't eat enough. It also helps if they don't drink too much. I have sat, sober and resentful, at so many of my own dinner-parties, wondering why on earth I took the trouble to make home-made ice cream and home-made biscuits when by that stage very few of the guests would notice whether the food was tinned or frozen.

The most obvious advantage of having greedy friends is that you feel less guilty about your own excesses. It is so depressing to eat with someone who is not really enthusiastic and who looks disdainfully at your loaded plate. Once I sat opposite a man at a dinner-party who looked at my extravagant helping of roast beef in disbelief and remarked: 'I can only assume you didn't have lunch.' My reply was truthful and defiant: 'Yes, and tea as well.'

There is an agreeable and instant bond between the truly greedy. A happily married couple I came across once admitted that, on their first dinner together, she had been unable to decide between one starter and another. After only a pretence at hesitation she ordered both. He did the same, and they realised they were dedicated gluttons. He tried to pretend that he only followed her example out of politeness, but he did not convince anyone.

There is an endearingly greedy heroine in Fay Weldon's novel *The Fat Woman's Joke*. She rebels against the monotony of preparing suitable meals for her prissy husband, and escapes to a basement in Earls Court to eat impressive amounts of baked beans, frozen chips and tinned suet pudding. This is infidelity of another calibre and breaks the self-imposed strictures of the sophisticated gourmet. These are that it is permissible to make a beast of yourself providing that the quality of the food is sufficiently superior. If you have made your own spaghetti and simmered the bolognese sauce for two hours, you are thoroughly justified in sprinkling it with freshly grated Parmesan, ignoring the absurd serving suggestion printed on the side of the packet, namely 2–3 ounces per person!

One of the most enjoyable aspects of infidelity in the kitchen is that the domestic rules laid down by even the most lenient husbands do not apply. Few men will agree to being a party to random eating through the day or night, and they don't seem to have the facility to eat bizarre food at inappropriate hours. I have a stepmother who has suffered from, or enjoyed (depending on your point of view), nocturnal pangs of hunger all her life. She and her husband were once pursued into their car by an

Infidelity in the Kitchen 65

Lady Camilla Dempster and friends

employee of the Ritz Hotel in Paris because she had left behind the supply of cheese that she had kept on the windowsill of her bedroom.

I have never been as greedy as to keep cheese on the bedroom windowsill during Nigel's absence – perhaps because I am greedy enough to go down three floors to the fridge to get it – or anything else I happen to have a craving for. In fact that probably increases the pleasure; after three flights and five minutes standing on a freezing floor trying to decide what to eat, the bliss of scurrying back to a warm bed with the spoils is total. There is only the cat to observe my abandoned greed, and she is well-fed too. No wonder I can say goodbye to Nigel so happily . . .

Eggs with sherry and orange (serves 2)

This recipe would be instantly rejected by my husband with the question 'Why would anyone mess about with perfectly good scrambled eggs?' Do not be put off by the inclusion of tomato ketchup; it makes the dish turn a delicate shade of coral, and it tastes better than you can imagine.

6 eggs
2 tablespoons sherry
3 tablespoons tomato ketchup
salt
cayenne pepper
butter
grated rind of 1 orange

Beat the eggs and sherry together. Add the tomato sauce. Season with salt and cayenne pepper. Melt some butter in a pan and pour in the mixture, stir until it begins to set, and sprinkle with grated rind of an orange. Decorate with croûtons.

Curry of turbot (serves 8)

Try to persuade the fishmonger to bone and skin the fish. He will think that you are wantonly extravagant but if you are inexperienced you won't be able to do it efficiently yourself and the amount of turbot you will have by the end of the operation will not satisfy anyone, greedy or not.

1½kg (3lb) turbot
3 medium onions
3 tablespoons curry powder
1 tablespoon wine vinegar
300ml (1pt) fresh tomato sauce
300ml (1pt) good stock
flour
150ml (¼pt) gill
fresh coriander and turmeric powder
oil for frying

Chop onions and fry in olive oil until light brown. Add curry powder, vinegar and the tomato sauce. Add chopped fresh coriander to the sauce. Take the turbot, boned, skinned and cut into pieces. Dip in flour and turmeric powder, and fry in olive oil until light brown. Remove and poach slowly in the curry, for 10 minutes. Add the cream before serving. Serve with plain boiled rice.

Mushroom coulibiac with herb sauce (serves 8)

180g (6oz) cooked rice (90g (3oz) raw rice)
370g (¾lb) mushrooms
½ lemon
2 × 400g (13oz) packets frozen puff pastry
1 egg yolk
3 eggs
60g (2oz) butter
90g (3oz) melted butter
salt and pepper

Herb sauce
120g (4oz) low-fat cream cheese
150ml (¼ pt) buttermilk
½ lemon
4 tablespoons chopped herbs: dill, tarragon, chives

Have the rice freshly boiled and well drained. Hard boil the eggs, shell and chop them. Slice the mushrooms thickly and cook gently in 60g (2oz) butter and lemon juice, in a covered pan for 12 minutes. Roll out the pastry into two squares. On one piece spread a layer of half the rice, mixed with the melted butter and seasoned with salt and pepper. Sprinkle over half the chopped eggs, then the mushrooms, drained of their juice. Cover with the remaining egg and the rest of the rice. Cover with the second piece of pastry and seal the edges firmly. Brush with the beaten egg yolk and bake for 25 minutes at 200°C/400°F, gas mark 6 until golden brown. Serve cold with a herb sauce.

Herb sauce
Put cheese and buttermilk in a blender until smooth. Add juice of the lemon, salt, pepper and herbs.

Hazelnut torte (serves 8)

120g (¼lb) hazelnuts
250g (½lb) Petit Beurre biscuits
120g (¼lb) sugar
2 whole eggs
2 egg yolks
150g (5oz) grated cooking chocolate
150g (5oz) butter

Toast the nuts in a moderate oven in a roasting tin for 8 minutes. Chop them in a blender. Wrap biscuits in a tea-towel, or in a paper bag, and crush them with a rolling-pin. Beat the sugar, eggs and yolks until they are light; this should take about 5 minutes. Add the chocolate and the melted butter to the egg mixture and cook in a double saucepan until it has thickened slightly; do not let it get too hot. Stir in nuts and biscuits. Pour the mixture into two well-buttered shallow cake tins or flan dishes, and when cool, chill. Serve with whipped cream.

Lady Margaret Douglas-Home

A Nostalgic Viennese Evening

I must explain how the recipes happened. My Austrian friend, Helga Mott, who later embarked on a serious and successful singing career, and I were steeped in the schmaltz of Viennese music. She sang waltzes enchantingly, and I became over-excited and sometimes inaccurate with the abandoned rhythm of the accompaniments. We tried them out on our long-suffering friends, usually after midnight; we told the BBC how good we were; they appeared to agree with us, but only put us on in the Children's Hour in a programme of sophisticated and unknown nursery rhymes. One hot afternoon, we dared to approach the office of a night club, heavily disguised in black wigs which would determine our anonymity in the event of our being accepted at the interview. We need not have worried.

Undeterred, we organised a party to be held in my house in Hampstead which would be a welcome escape from frustration and reticence. Our husbands were decorative and essential ingredients for it. They were good-looking, unmistakable Englishmen, bowler hats at the ready for the morning. The magic of the evening came from the Viennese band, authentic in every way, led by a small stocky Maestro who arrived breathlessly late. He and Helga began, and for the next six hours we never left the enchantment of Vienna. We danced and danced, and the Pilsner began to bring out the mood of golden content, after the Imperial Tokay had jolted us out of our native apathy: the legendary Tokay, said to have brought the Austrian Imperial family back to life (they badly needed it).

The Maestro forgot his beautiful silk scarf when he left, and I still have it in my

possession. The Maestro never claimed it, seemed to have no address, and the men of my family used to wear it sometimes on important occasions.

At the end of the party the unravelling of the cars on a narrow hill outside took some time. An elderly high-ranking soldier had danced more energetically and without doubt more beautifully than anyone else (he had spent most of his twenties in Vienna). He was struggling with his car lock, being instructed by a policeman through the open window. The soldier was still in the world of schmaltz and Pilsner, and he said 'Thank you, Willis'. Then he looked at the policeman for the first time, who stared back at him, and stood at ease. And it *was* Willis! They had not met since they were in the same platoon in the Great War; they had not known if the other was still alive. The re-establishing of that friendship had to be properly done, and it was quite morning before the army left us.

I doubt if Viennese cookery has changed much since those days. I found our party dishes in several contemporary cookery books, and they seemed to need as many eggs, and as much cream and preparation as before the War. Sometimes I have crucified the Kastanienberg by using a tube of chestnut purée, and it was *delicious*.

The library of books which litters my kitchen helps to trigger off ideas – usually I concentrate on the cakes and soufflés sections, as these are my passions. I have no natural flair or even natural common sense (I understand many of my contemporaries also feel the lack of both). As I have never had a formal education in gastronomy, it is still hit or miss. One remembers the misses long afterwards. Now that I no longer have to provide regular meals, I go to town when the grandchildren appear – at the risk of upsetting their parents over their 'brown rice' regimes. It used to be so hard trying to make each meal unordinary when one was cooking constantly every day, but it was really a relief to all my generation after the crunch had come and there was no alternative but to jolly well do it oneself. And, on the whole, the food was better than the pretty nasty meals produced by the staff. But even now the finished products do not look as right as when Mrs Reeves was in command of her regiment of underlings. (God bless her memory and her apple charlotte.)

Apfelstrudel with short pastry

Prepare a short pastry, working quickly with:
155g (5oz) flour
a pinch of salt
90g (3oz) butter
90g (3oz) sugar
yolk of a small egg
2 tablespoons white wine

Leave in a cool place for at least one hour.

Then for the filling mix together:
500g (1lb) cooking apples
75g (2½oz) sugar
30g (1oz) sultanas
1 egg white
a little rum or lemon juice

Roll out the pastry into an oblong sheet. Cover the middle with apple mixture. Fold over pastry from either end, brushing with egg white and pinching the ends together. Brush the top of the strudel with egg white too. Bake for at least 30 minutes at 200°C/400°F, gas mark 6. Dust lightly with sugar. Leave to cool.

Kastanienberg mit Schlagrahm

2 tablespoons chocolate
5 eggs
1 cup sugar
2 cups cooked and mashed chestnuts

Melt the chocolate in a double boiler. Beat the egg whites until stiff. Fold in the sugar, egg yolks and chestnuts. Grease a pudding mould and sprinkle with sugar. Steam, covered with foil, for 1 hour.

Serve with
1 cup heavy cream
2 tablespoons sugar
1¼ cups chestnuts, cooked and mashed, mixed with sugar.

Jagdwecken

5 anchovies
1½ cups butter
3 small pickles, diced
1kg (2lb) smoked tongue, cooked and diced
1 cup ham, diced
1 cup Edam cheese, diced
2 tablespoons mock caviar
2 loaves french bread 14 inches long

Rub anchovies through strainer. Blend with butter, pickles, tongue, ham, cheese and caviar. Scoop out bread. Stuff with filling. Keep in a cool place.

Sachertorte

155g (5oz) vanilla chocolate, or ordinary chocolate with a drop of vanilla essence
1 dessertspoon water
155g (5oz) butter
6 eggs
155g (5oz) powdered sugar
155g (5oz) flour (well sifted)
apricot jam
chocolate icing

Melt the chocolate with the water over a gentle heat. Stir well and add butter, beating it into the chocolate. Add egg yolks, sugar, then whip until frothy. Beat the egg whites until stiff and add alternately with the flour to the chocolate mixture. Cook in a sandwich tin in even heat. When the cake is cooked and cooled, spread with an apricot glaze, and ice with chocolate icing.

Rose Elliot

A Vegetarian Harvest Festival

One of the most challenging entertaining feats I have undertaken was a harvest supper for a hundred and fifty people. I was at that time working for the religious charity which my family runs, and the harvest supper was originally planned as a simple meal for about fifty people returning from a day's sponsored walk over the Downs. However, such was the enthusiasm with which the idea of the supper was received that we decided to open it to other people as well. Entry was by tickets, which we sold in advance, priced to cover the cost of the food with some profit on top for the charity funds. In the end we found ourselves catering for a hundred and fifty guests, about two-thirds of whom came just for the supper.

The event took place on the last Saturday in September, and the supper was held in three adjoining rooms in a large house. We cleared away most of the furniture, putting the chairs round the sides, and trestle tables down the centre for the food. We decorated the rooms and the tables with autumn flowers and leaves in shades of gold, orange and brown, and picked up the orange in the napkins and candles. Given the numbers coming to the supper, we had to borrow china and knives and forks and these had to be counted and listed. I was glad that this side of things was taken care of by my sister and two other friends.

My chief concern was with the food. Obviously we were restricted to dishes which could be prepared in large quantities in advance and be simple to serve, so that people could help themselves and eat standing up with just a fork. It also had to be vegetarian, since that was the preference of most of the guests. But as I am vegetarian myself that wasn't a problem. My main difficulty lay in trying to provide food which would appeal equally to the walkers, who were tired and hungry and just wanting something simple and soothing, and to those who were coming just for the supper and wanting something more exciting.

I decided to start with pumpkin soup, served with warm wholewheat rolls and hot garlic bread. The soup seemed perfectly in keeping with the harvest theme, an attractive gold-orange in colour and gloriously smooth and creamy. We hollowed out the pumpkin skins to make Hallowe'en-style lanterns to decorate the rooms: enough, in retrospect, to give the local fire-prevention officer nightmares, but luckily with no ill-effects.

The rest of the food was planned on the salads-and-quiche format, with a choice of gâteaux, meringues and fruity puddings. I made moist savoury nut loaves well in advance and froze them, so that they only needed de-freezing and slicing. Flans I always make fresh, as I do not consider these freeze well. So I cooked the pastry cases on the Friday and filled and baked them in batches on the day of the supper so that the pastry was crisp and some of them were still warm.

I chose mainly salads which could be prepared the day before and would keep perfectly, covered with clingfilm in a cool place. They included a colourful cabbage salad, rice and vegetable salad, potato salad and cucumber and yogurt salad. Lettuce and watercress were also washed the day before and kept in polythene bags in the bottom of the fridge to become crisp: these were then arranged around the nut loaf. The one salad I did make on the day was tomato and avocado.

The puddings, too, were largely made in advance. The most popular one consisted of blackberries and cooking apples, cooked separately without water, cooled, then layered into a glass serving dish and covered with lightly whipped cream and crushed roasted hazel nuts. This was served with meringues, and I also made some chocolate biscuit gâteaux and several coffee meringue gâteaux: this last is useful because not only can the meringue circles be made well in advance, but, unlike most meringue gâteaux, can be assembled the day before.

The big problem when catering for large numbers is always the quantity of food to prepare. For 150 we made 6 gallons of soup; I allowed a slice of flan and a slice of nut loaf per person, so we made 25 flans and 20 nut loaves. Salads were more difficult to judge, and the first time I catered for the supper I experimented with quantities beforehand, reckoning that every guest would have a spoonful of each type of salad and counting to see how many spoonfuls a given quantity would produce, then multiplying up. After this I just kept notes of quantities and ingredients from year to year. In general I found that a salad which would normally serve 4 people was enough for 10–12 people when served at a buffet supper with other salads.

The first year I made a mistake over the quantities of puddings. I offered several different types which together added up to a total of about 150 portions. I did not allow for the fact that quite a few people would try more than one, and I am afraid that some people went without that year. I found that for 150 people we needed to allow about 375 portions of pudding.

A Vegetarian Harvest Festival

As far as drinks were concerned, we offered a choice of grape juice or dry white wine, and coffee to finish the meal.

All this entailed a good deal of effort, and I was glad to have the help of three friends who worked with me from the Thursday before and also helped with the clearing up afterwards. A number of other people helped for shorter periods or did specific jobs, such as the friend who spent the week before making batches of meringues (saving the yolks for my flans), and another who popped in at regular intervals to make cups of tea and coffee for the rest of the helpers.

The supper was very successful and, as you will have gathered, became an annual event: I catered for it for seven years in succession and have happy memories of preparation and evenings alike.

Pumpkin soup (serves 6)

Makes 1.4 litres (3 pints):
1kg (2¼lb) pumpkin (this weight includes the skin and pips)
2 large onions
2 large cloves of garlic
25g (1oz) butter
1 litre (1¾pt) stock
sea salt
freshly ground black pepper
150ml (5fl oz) single cream or top of the milk

Peel the pumpkin and scoop out the seeds; cut the flesh into even-sized pieces. Peel and chop the onion; peel and crush the garlic.

Melt the butter in a heavy saucepan and cook the chopped onions for about 5 minutes, then put in the garlic and pumpkin and cook for a further 5 minutes. Add the stock and some salt and pepper; bring to the boil and simmer until the pumpkin is tender – this takes about 15 or 20 minutes. Sieve or liquidise the soup, then stir in the single cream or top of the milk. Reheat the soup gently. Serve in individual bowls with hot garlic bread or warm wholewheat rolls.

Onion and soured cream flan with wholewheat pastry (serves 8)

This is a good flan with a creamy filling and crisp base, and it conveniently uses up egg yolks left over from making meringues or the meringue gâteau below.

175g (6oz) plain wholewheat flour
pinch of salt
75g (3oz) butter
1 egg yolk

Filling
350g (12oz) onion, peeled and chopped
25g (1oz) butter
150ml (5fl oz) soured cream
2 egg yolks
sea salt, freshly ground black pepper and grated nutmeg

Set the oven to 200°C/400°F, gas mark 6. If possible place a baking sheet in the oven to heat up: standing the flan dish on this helps the bottom of the flan to cook crisply. Sift the flour and salt into a bowl, adding also the residue of bran from the sieve. Rub in the butter until the mixture looks like fine breadcrumbs, then mix in the egg yolk and a very small quantity of cold water if necessary to make a smooth dough. Roll out thinly to line a 23cm (9-inch) flan tin. Prick the base lightly and bake in the preheated oven for 15 minutes to cook the pastry. (The flan can be cooled at this point and stored in a tin overnight if more convenient.)

Turn the oven setting down to 180°C/350°F, gas mark 4.

To make the filling, fry the onion in the butter for 10 minutes, until softened but not browned. Remove from the heat, then stir in the cream and egg yolks, and season with salt, pepper and grated nutmeg. Pour into the flan and bake for about 30 minutes, until the filling is set.

Savoury nut loaf (cuts into 8 slices)

For chopping the nuts and vegetables I find an autochop gives the best results, producing just the right amount of chewy texture. But some form of electric grater or food processor is essential if you are going to make this recipe in any quantity, as I did for the harvest supper.

butter and dried crumbs for preparing the tin
1 large onion, peeled and chopped
1 medium-sized carrot, scraped and chopped
1 small stick of celery, chopped
25g (1oz) butter
1 tablespoon wholewheat flour
100ml (4fl oz) water
½ teaspoon mixed herbs
175g (6oz) mixed nuts: almonds, cashew nuts or hazel nuts, including some walnuts
1–2 teaspoons Marmite
75g (3oz) soft wholewheat breadcrumbs
2 eggs
sea salt
freshly ground black pepper

Set the oven to 180°C/350°F, gas mark 4. Prepare a 450g (1lb) loaf tin by lining with a strip of silicone (non-stick) paper, greasing generously with butter and sprinkling with a thick layer of dried breadcrumbs: this helps the loaf to turn out intact and also makes the outside crisp.

Fry the vegetables in the butter for 10 minutes until tender and slightly browned; add the flour, then add the water and stir until very thick. Remove from the heat and mix in the nuts, herbs, Marmite, breadcrumbs, eggs and seasoning. Spoon the mixture into the prepared tin. Bake, uncovered, for 1 hour, until the top is firm to the touch and lightly browned.

It can be served hot, as a vegetarian main course, or cooled, sliced and served with salads. Some creamy lemon mayonnaise goes very well with it.

Coffee meringue gâteau with chocolate filling (serves 8)

4 egg whites
225g (8oz) castor sugar
1 tablespoon good quality instant coffee powder

Filling
150g (6oz) dark chocolate
150g (6oz) unsalted butter
50g (2oz) castor sugar

Set the oven to 120°C/250°F, gas mark ½. Line three baking trays with greaseproof paper, then draw a 23 cm (9-inch) diameter circle on each. Brush the greaseproof paper thoroughly with cooking oil. Whisk the egg whites until they are stiff, then whisk in half the sugar and the instant coffee. Fold in the rest of the sugar with a metal spoon. Divide the meringue between the three baking sheets, spreading it to fit the circles. Bake for 2–3 hours, until the meringue is completely dry and crisp. Cool completely, then strip off the greaseproof paper.

To make the filling, break the chocolate into pieces, reserving two pieces for the garnish. Put the rest into a bowl and melt over a pan of hot water. Cream together the butter and sugar, then add the melted chocolate and beat again. Leave for 30 minutes or so, until it has thickened to a spreadable consistency. Place one meringue circle on a serving dish and spread with half the butter cream; repeat with another circle and the remaining butter cream, then put the final circle on top, and press it down gently. Grate the reserved chocolate over the top. Leave in a cool place until the butter cream is firm: this gâteau can be covered lightly with foil and kept in a cool place overnight.

Jane Grigson

A Summer Lunch

It was not by intention that I began to write about food. My aim had been to spend a quiet life in the Victoria and Albert Museum, studying painting or antique silver or textiles. Instead I found myself in a seventeenth-century farmhouse kitchen. It had no hot running water or a refrigerator and was dominated by a temperamental Esse Fairy. So heavily did this object weigh on my inexperience that even today I regard a soufflé which rises as a kind of miracle. If there were an altar to the god Thermostat, with his handmaid, the kitchen timer, I should make a pilgrimage to it yearly.

Gradually things changed. We acquired a dishwasher to avoid arguments with teenage children, then a refrigerator, then a floor polisher so that the old stone flags began to shine and reflect the light. The wall rotted between the kitchen and the room where they once made Wiltshire cheese. It was knocked down and the kitchen became twice as large, the family room that we had always wanted to have, where children could crawl and play in safety, or splash food from their high chairs, do their homework, tell their troubles and share their triumphs. Everyone congregates in the kitchen to drink and talk, perching on stools or window-seat amidst the general muddle. In the centre is a huge table. One of my best memories is of a visit from Ben Nicholson. He would sit on the other side of the table and talk to me, while I chopped and peeled. He liked the artistry of cooking, though he ate little himself except for fish and vegetables and puddings (he gave me a recipe for brown bread ice cream). He took to the kitchen so much that he turned me out one whole day so that

A scholar cook

he could have it to himself and draw a glass goblet he had bought in Bath. I suppose we picnicked in the garden at lunchtime.

It is this association of food with friends and every aspect of existence that makes me happy to be a food writer. Painting, history, archaeology, architecture, the way the countryside and town worked together in the past, where foods have come from, what the best writers and painters liked to eat, what the great cooks thought about their trade – all these things make the study of what we eat the least boring of occupations. No aspect of my life has been untouched by it. Through it I have made many friends, read and seen things, visited places that I had never even hoped to know about when I was young.

Of course the work is absorbing. The winter is devoted to it. We see few friends, work every day. Then spring comes. We set off for our very small cave house on the northern border of Touraine, return to a garden with the roses coming out, then go back to France for the season of melons and peaches and the first apples. It is the time to entertain the people we like best, family and colleagues, whole families sitting outdoors in the shade of a medlar or apple or lime tree.

I choose food that is crisp and piquant, a large sheet of pastry covered with onion and tomato, anchovies, olives and slices of mozzarella added at the end of cooking time so that it just melts without turning to strings. Hot weather means less meat: Bayonne or Parma ham, smoked chicken, some good boiled ham or a chicken livened with shellfish is my limit. Vast joints are revolting in the sun, so are creamy ragouts and fricassees. Fish is another matter: whole salmon trout, cool silver and pink, or steamed John Dory with mayonnaise in the Venetian style. When I can get hold of such things, a vast dish of seafood is my choice – crabs, lobsters, prawns, mussels, oysters and winkles – such things take hours to eat, which makes for relaxed conversation, and stomachs cannot be overloaded at that slow rate.

Cool aspects of the meal might be a chilled melon soup, from melon liquidised with soured cream: I keep an empty water melon shell in the freezer to act as tureen, and put it on a bed of bay leaves. To drink we have local sauvignons in France, with Beaumes de Venise for the dessert course; in England, a white Rioja that we have taken to lately, and a choice of Kir or Cardinale as apéritif since I usually have some crème de cassis made from blackcurrants grown at our village fruit farm. Kir is cassis, a very little, plus white wine, and Cardinale is cassis with red wine. Another drink I love in summer is the Indian lassi, equal quantities of yogurt and water liquidised to a foaming froth, with some cream, then salted and chilled; when we come to drink it, I put a pinch of cumin seed on top, or a leaf or two of mint. It is just right with spiced food, or as a cooling drink on its own.

Anchoïade de Croze (serves 8)

This elaborate version of a Provençal *anchoïade* comes from one of the leaders of the regional cookery movement that began to be strong in the Twenties. The ingredients sound strange, the result is strong like a *tapénade*, but magical, especially on a hot day. With a processor it can be made in minutes.

small dried hot red pepper (chilli)
12 blanched almonds
12 anchovies in oil or 1¾oz tin
12 anchovies in brine, washed, boned
3 dried figs, cut up roughly
small onion, quartered
2 cloves of garlic, quartered
2 good sprigs of green fennel
60g (2oz) mixed parsley, chives, tarragon
olive oil
lemon juice
about a tablespoon orangeflower water
24 small bridge rolls and black olives

Process the solid ingredients together to a paste, dripping in about 4 tablespoons of olive oil to start with, then extras as needed, alternating with lemon juice to taste. Finally add the orangeflower water, stopping to sample the *anchoïade* every so often: orangeflower water can be bossy out of proportion to the quantity.

Cut open the rolls. Remove a little crumb from the top. Fill with *anchoïade*, and brush the lower cut side with oil. Close and arrange on a baking sheet, brushing the rolls with oil. Bake at 200–220°C/400–425°F, gas mark 6–7, for about 10 minutes until slightly crisp and hot through. Serve with black olives.

If you do not have a baker who can provide bridge rolls, put the *anchoïade* in a bowl and serve it with hot fingers of bread, roughly cut, brushed with oil and baked in the oven.

Clear soup royale (serves 6–8)

One of the great treats – for me, at any rate – is a clear soup with an egg and cream *royale*. Not difficult to make, but it needs care to ensure that the liquid never boils.

750g–1kg (1½–2lb) shoulder fillet of beef or other cut near the blade bone
4 turkey wing tips, *ie* the two end sections of the wing
250g (8oz) poultry giblets, excluding liver
beef marrow bone or veal knuckle
onion in its skin, quartered
2–3 medium carrots, quartered
1 leek or 2 young green-stemmed onions or 6 spring onions
4 cloves garlic
2 tomatoes, halved and grilled (optional)
1 tablespoon peppercorns
bouquet garni

The royale
3 large eggs or 2 yolks and 2 eggs
2 tablespoons double cream
1 tablespoon soured cream
pepper and salt

Put all the meat into a huge pot and pour over plenty of water to cover it generously – measure what you put in and do not go beyond a litre for every half kilo.

Bring slowly to simmering point; skim well, tip in a mug of cold water and skim again. Repeat if necessary. When clear, add the remaining ingredients. Adjust the stove so that the liquid moves and gives an occasional bubble but never boils, or it will become murky.

After 4–5 hours, remove enough of the liquid to give you the quantity of soup you require. If the beef is tender, you can make a lunch of it with the poultry bits and pieces. Or you can leave it to cool for a meal later on. Or you can top up the liquid and go on drawing off the stock as long as the meat has any virtue left in it; if you have a deep-freeze this is a sensible thing to do.

For the soup, add salt and a few drops of lemon juice, then pour it through a double muslin into a pan for reheating. You can add alcohol, reduce, if you must, but I like it best without.

For the garnish, beat egg and creams with seasoning. Butter a shallow pan and steam until it is firm. Turn out and cut into dice or small shapes with a cutter and serve in the soup. If you value firm clear-cut shapes, steam the mixture until it is quite solid; if you like a milder creaminess and do not mind a ragged edge or two, steam it until it just stops shaking in the centre.

Cucumber mousse and passion fruit sorbet

Cucumber mousse (serves 8)

When people drop in on a Sunday evening, on their way back to town, this is a good thing to serve on a warm day. Not heavy but, with wholemeal bread and white wine or Perrier to drink, sustaining and refreshing.

½ large cucumber, peeled, diced small
heaped teaspoon salt
3 tablespoons tarragon vinegar
1 packet 15g (½oz) gelatine
300ml (½pt) whipping or double cream
500g (1lb) curd cheese or ricotta *or* 250g (8oz) each sieved cottage and cream cheese
black pepper
plenty of chopped chives, parsley, spring onion

Mix cucumber, salt and vinegar thoroughly in a basin. Then turn into a colander, put a plate on top and leave to drain for an hour at least. Remove the plate and press with a cloth, not too hard.

Dissolve gelatine in 6 tablespoons of very hot water, cool to tepid and whisk in the cream gradually until the mixture is smooth and very thick but not stiff. Mash the cheese with a fork if necessary so that it mixes evenly with the cream. It should not be too smooth in texture. Add the cucumber. Taste and add a shade more vinegar and salt if absolutely necessary, but be careful not to make the taste too strong. Grind in black pepper, then stir in the herbs. Turn into an oiled mould and leave overnight to set.

Tomato cream (serves 6)

I use this cream as a centrepiece and surround it with salad greenery, hard-boiled eggs and prawns or crab with slivers of chicken.

tomatoes
gelatine
250ml (8fl oz) whipping cream
salt
cayenne pepper
sugar

Skin, process and sieve enough well-flavoured tomatoes to give you 425ml (14fl oz). Mix in gelatine dissolved as above, then flavour with salt, ½ teaspoon of cayenne and a little sugar. The taste should be strong as cream will mute it. Chill until the mixture has an egg-white consistency. Fold in 250ml (8fl oz) whipping cream, beaten until stiff but not rigid. Check seasoning. Set in a decorative mould, brushed with oil, overnight.

Lemon chicken (serves 6)

In the North we sneer sometimes at the idea of tepid food, but when the weather turns hot there is a good deal to be said for it – as the Greeks know well. With tepid food you get more flavour and less stodginess than with cold. Certainly it is the case with chicken, or guineafowl, which are the only uncured meats I find tolerable on a hot day.

1 large chicken
1 lemon
150ml (¼pt) giblet, light beef or veal stock
90g (3oz) butter
pepper
salt
new potatoes
parsley and chive butter
crisp-leaved lettuce

Sauce
grated zest and juice of a large lemon
4 large egg yolks
250g (8oz) lightly salted Danish or unsalted butter
salt and pepper

Ease skin round the cavity opening of the bird, then work your fingers gently until it is completely raised from the breast meat and top of the legs. Scrub the lemon, cut off and discard the ends, then slice the rest thinly (getting rid of the pips). Cut away most of the surrounding skin and pith, leaving just enough to hold the frail slices together. Slip them in under the skin, patterning the chicken as well as you can. All the slices may not be needed – keep them for a final decoration.

Either roast the chicken with the stock in the dish, after spreading it with the butter. Or put the stock into a pot on top of the stove and add lightly browned chicken (use the butter), cover and cook gently, turning it from time to time: this is a better way of cooking meat in warm weather as it avoids overheating the kitchen. Meanwhile steam the new potatoes and turn them in the herb butter. Arrange them on a dish and keep warm.

The sauce is a form of hollandaise. Put the zest and half the juice of the lemon, with the egg yolks, into a saucepan, liquidiser or processor. Melt the butter and gradually whisk it into the yolks bubbling hot first. Taste and add more lemon juice if you like, though the flavour should not be overwhelming. Alternatively, cook it in a double boiler as for hollandaise.

When the chicken is done, put it on the dish and boil down the liquid. Add some to the sauce, if you like, pour the rest over the chicken: there should not be very much of it. Cut the lettuce into shreds. Skim fat from the roasting juices and consider their flavour. Boil them down if they are on the weak side. Otherwise just bring them to the boil and pour them over the chicken: they wilt the lettuce very slightly, making a warm salad in the French style which is delicious with the chicken. Place the lettuce and potatoes around the bird in alternating mounds. Serve the sauce separately.

Passion fruit sorbet (serves 8)

After years of beating and refreezing and hovering over ices as anxiously as if they were soufflés, I have taken refuge in an ice-making machine that works painlessly – the Ice Cream Man. You tip in the mixture when you start the cheese course, or half-way through the main course, and in 20 minutes you have an ice of perfect texture, smooth, coherent, without flinty chips of ice. This recipe can of course be made by any of the other methods – it takes extra trouble, that is all.

8 passion fruits
2 limes
2 cups of sugar

Measure 2 cups of sugar and 2 cups of water into a pan – I take a cup to be 250ml (8fl oz) but in the case of this recipe it does not have to be exactly that. Dissolve them together, bring to the boil and simmer for 5 minutes.

Meanwhile scoop the pulp from 8 passion fruits into another pan. Pour on half the hot syrup and set over a low heat until the flesh loosens round the seeds. Sieve into a basin, pushing through all the flesh you can. Keep half the seeds.

With a zester, remove the zest of 2 limes in fine shreds and set aside. Or cut off zest thinly, slice into julienne strips and simmer until tender, in water.

Squeeze the limes. Add this juice and the remaining syrup alternately to the passion fruit, until you get the flavour you like. Passion fruit vary in strength and acidity, which means you cannot be precise as to the quantity of lime juice or syrup required. Mix in the seeds, leaving a teaspoonful.

Freeze in a machine according to its instructions, or in the deep-freeze. When solid all round but liquid in the centre, remove and beat with an electric whisk until foamy. Refreeze, and beat again if necessary.

Serve in glasses, the ice topped with lime shreds and a few black seeds.

Pamela Harlech

Preserves and Pickles

During July, August and September my life in the country is totally centred around the fresh fruit and vegetables coming in from the garden. The soft fruit, such as gooseberries, black and white currants, raspberries and finally blackberries, are made into jams, jellies and conserves. Indeed, in the summer, a muslin jelly bag and stand is set up permanently in the middle of the kitchen table. Whenever anyone goes out for a walk, I give them one of a variety of baskets bought despite my husband's pleading protests in Greece, Portugal, France and Spain. Then comes the order, 'On your way back, please fill this with whatever fruit is ripe.' The fruit is either made into jam or softened with a few pints of water and poured into the jelly bag. Excess fruit is flash-frozen on trays in the freezer, then put into 1lb plastic bags for use throughout the winter.

Cucumbers are brought in from the greenhouse at just the right ripeness for pickling, and in early September the damsons are picked by a family onslaught on four burgeoning trees; as are the sloes at the end of September. I prefer Damson Vodka to Sloe Gin, but make both to give as Christmas presents to great friends. As a result, there are three or four steady customers who are champing at the bit around the beginning of December, but I insist on waiting until the last possible moment to decant the deep burgundy liqueur into the very pretty bottles which have been collected throughout the year.

I also have damson addicts who gobble up all the damson cheese, jam and conserve.

In January, after a few months' rest, it is time to make marmalades – as a kindness to my family. I say this with a halo glowing over my head because I am one of the few people in the world who loathe marmalade of any kind!

There are certain rules which should be followed for any kind of pickling, preserving of jam, or jelly-making. It is *essential* to sterilise the jars into which the mixture will be put. Sterilisation means the destruction of all enemy organisms by a thorough application of moist heat produced by boiling water or steam. If you are bottling fruit or vegetables, you must boil them for a certain stated period according to the individual recipe after the food is placed in the jars.

To sterilise the empty jars or bottles: after thoroughly washing them, place them and their tops or covers in enough warm water to cover them. Bring them to boiling point and allow them to boil for at least 15 minutes. Remove each jar from the boiling water as it is needed for filling, or allow them to drain on a rack in the second warmest oven in the Aga. Remove the tops or covers from the water only when they are to be placed on the jars. If the tops have rubber sealers, boil them in a separate utensil for fifteen minutes.

There are four types of foods which belong to the group ordinarily known as preserves: jams and jellies, conserves, marmalades, and fruit butters. All contain a large amount of sugar in proportion to the amount of juice and pulp, although I use less sugar than usually suggested because I prefer a slightly tart to an over-sweet taste.

In many cases the pulp remaining from the fruit used in making jelly may be utilised in the making of jams, butters or conserves. The difference between a jam and a butter is that a butter is made from large fruit, *ie* apples, peaches, plums, pears, which do not contain small seeds, while a jam is made from small berry type fruit.

Marmalade is different from jam because it is not necessary for jam to gel, whereas marmalade should always be of a jelly-like consistency and should contain fruit in large enough pieces to be easily distinguished. Marmalade can be made with a combination of four or five different citrus fruits. A conserve proper is a happy medium between a jam and a marmalade, frequently consisting of a combination of fruits such as rhubarb and orange, or grape and apple, with or without the addition of other solid ingredients like raisins or nuts. It is always richer than a jam or marmalade, and more solid in consistency.

There are a few hints which are important before embarking upon a session of pickling and preserving. Most important is to prevent discoloration in jellies, preserves or relishes, so always use enamelled or stainless steel cooking utensils, never aluminium. Then, since green fruit contains more natural pectin than fully ripe fruit, the juice should be tested before the jelly stage. Nearly one quarter of the fruit you are going to use should be semi-green. Make a test juice of 1 tablespoon (15ml) fruit juice, 1 teaspoon (5ml) sugar, and 1½ teaspoons (7.5ml) Epsom salts. Put the juice into a small glass and mix the rest of the ingredients until they dissolve, let it set for 20 minutes, then stir it again. If gelatinous particles form, it contains enough pectin; if not, add 1 or 2 tablespoons (15–30ml) of lemon juice to each 225ml (8fl oz) of fruit juice before making the jelly. Be sure to pour the test juice away.

The recipes I have included here are particular favourites of mine and are slightly outside the ordinary.

Grape fudge conserve (makes 4 1lb jars)

1.5kg (3lb) washed green grapes
225ml (8 fl oz) water
1kg (2lb) granulated sugar
grated rind and juice of 1 lemon and 1 orange
250g (½lb) chopped walnuts
250g (½lb) raisins

Peel the grapes, reserving the skins. Place the peeled grapes and water in a saucepan and heat slowly over a low heat until the grapes turn soft and pulpy. Meanwhile chop up the grape skins and raisins. Pour the grape pulp through a strainer, rubbing gently with a wooden spoon so that all the seeds are left behind. Return the grapes to the saucepan, add the sugar and raisins, and simmer over a low fire for about 30 minutes until the mixture thickens. Add the orange and lemon rind and juice and simmer for a further 5 minutes. Stir in the nuts at the last minute. Pour into heated, sterilised jam jars, seal and cool. Let the preserve rest for at least 2 months before using it.

Fresh basil jelly (makes 5 225ml (8 fl oz) jelly-glasses)

This is particularly delicious served with game, but also a treat with lamb or cold chicken. Usually one makes an apple jelly base and adds the basil to this, but I find that this does not give a strong enough taste of basil to the jelly. So for this jelly you must use commercial pectin, such as Certo.

90g (3oz) fresh basil leaves, picked over and
    thoroughly cleaned
10 fresh basil leaves reserved for garnish
500ml (16fl oz) water
150ml (6fl oz) basil vinegar
50ml (2fl oz) lemon juice
1.5kg (3lb) preserving or granulated sugar
5 drops green food colouring
90ml (6 tablespoons) Certo

In a large enamel or stainless steel saucepan, boil together the water, vinegar and lemon juice. Bruise the basil leaves and add them to the boiling liquid. Remove from the heat and allow the mixture to infuse for 10 minutes. Then add the sugar and colouring. Return the mixture to the heat and boil, stirring constantly, until the sugar dissolves. When the syrup is at a full rolling boil, add the Certo. Boil for 30 seconds, then remove from the heat. Place 2 fresh basil leaves in each sterilized jar, then strain the jelly into the jelly glasses through a fine sieve. Cool to room temperature. Clean away any excess jelly from the top of the glass and seal.

Jerusalem artichoke relish (makes 8–10 pint-jars)

2kg (4lb) Jerusalem artichokes
1kg (2lb) onions, chopped fine
6 bell green peppers, chopped fine
2 cauliflower heads, broken into small flowerets
4.2 litres (1 gallon) water
225g (½lb) salt
75g (2½oz) flour
225g (½lb) sugar
30ml (2 tablespoons) dry mustard
15ml (1 tablespoon) turmeric
2.4 litres (4pts) white vinegar
120g (4oz) chopped pimentos
15ml (1 tablespoon) mustard seed
10ml (2 teaspoons) celery seed

Scrub and chop the artichokes. Add the onions, peppers and cauliflower. Soak the mixture overnight in water with salt. Drain well in colander and rinse with clear water.

Mix the flour, sugar, mustard and turmeric and add vinegar to make a paste. Heat the remaining vinegar in a large roaster or preserving kettle and add the paste mixture. Cook for about 5 minutes to blend. Add the vegetables, pimento, mustard seed and celery seed, and bring to the boil. Seal in pint jars.

Bread and butter pickles (about 9½ pints – 12 jam jars)

14 medium cucumbers, unpeeled, sliced thin
9 medium onions, sliced thin
2 fresh chilli peppers or 4 dried peppers
120g (4oz) salt
1250g (2½lb) sugar
7.5ml (1½ teaspoons) turmeric
10ml (2 teaspoons) mustard seed
5ml (1 teaspoon) celery seed
2.5ml (½ teaspoon) ground cloves

Take a large enamel soup pot (not aluminium because of the vinegar), and put the cucumbers, then the onions in alternate layers until you have filled the pot. Cut up the peppers and place them on top. Sprinkle salt over the mixture, cover it all with ice, and allow it to stand for 3 hours. Then pour off the water, add the sugar, vinegar and seasoning. Mix well with your hands. Then simmer the pickle mixture over low heat for 15–20 minutes until the rind turns brown. *Do not allow it to boil.* Seal in sterilised jars while hot. Leave for at least 4 months before eating, if you can stand the wait!

Summer bottled

Damson gin or vodka (makes about 1 litre (2 pints))

500g (1lb) damsons, washed
120g (4oz) granulated sugar
1.2 litres (2pts) gin or vodka
2.5ml ($\frac{1}{4}$ teaspoon) almond essence

With a tapestry needle, prick each damson about 5 times, to allow the juices to run out. Take a large glass container – large enough to hold all the liquid plus the damsons and sugar – and put the damsons, sugar, gin or vodka and almond essence into this. (Keep the empty gin or vodka bottles.) Put on the top of the container, give it a good shake, then lay it on its side. Once a week for 3 months, shake it, then turn it and lay it on its side. At the end of 3 months, put a funnel into the original gin or vodka bottles, or any other pretty bottle you may have, and syphon the liquid into them. You may then place the damsons into a jar, cover them with some fresh gin or vodka, and eat them as liqueur fruit. They are also delicious used in puddings. The longer you keep the liquid in the original bottle, the stronger the fruit taste.

This recipe may also be used for sloe gin or vodka, substituting sloes for the damsons.

Lady Holborow

A Feast Fit for Judges

I first came to Cornwall when I married 23 years ago. I had never done any cooking and was apprehensive about starting. My husband says the only time I ever stopped talking was during the last few days of our honeymoon when I started worrying about how I was going to cope in our kitchen! My mother gave me a pre-war cookery book called *Dinners for Beginners* which, together with a copy of Constance Spry, was given to every bride in those days. These two books were my teachers in my early married days. We lived at Feock then, by the sea, and had a stone-flagged kitchen, an old enamel sink and wooden draining board, and a brand-new electric cooker. We have moved since, and I now have a large kitchen with most modern gadgets. Rather to my regret, I have never had an Aga.

Looking back, the main problem I used to have was buying the ingredients for the recipes I wanted to use. I could not buy veal; peppers, aubergines and avocado pears were practically unobtainable; and the only cream available was clotted, and I was looked at askance if I asked for what was known as 'raw cream'. In fact I had to buy a cream-making machine to be able to use whipped cream in any form. I can remember the excitement when a delicatessen opened in Truro and I was able to buy spices, sour cream, yogurt and tins of red peppers! Things have changed now; Truro is a very good shopping town, and we even have Marks and Spencer! Being near the sea, the fish has always been excellent. There is nothing to beat freshly caught mackerel or shell fish.

We have always had a vegetable garden, and I really enjoy picking my own vegetables and seeing the first of the peas, beans and potatoes coming through the ground. In the mild climate of Cornwall we are able to have early potatoes grown

outdoors from the middle of May, and there is nothing more delicious than a potato or any vegetable which has only been dug up or picked an hour or so before.

My cooking has always been spasmodic, and I prefer to have sessions in the kitchen every few weeks rather than committing myself to an hour or two every day. Living in Cornwall, we have relatively quiet winters, with small dinner-parties of Cornish friends, and summers inundated with guests either staying with us or holidaying nearby and visiting us for meals. Some years we have clocked up over 100 visitors in our Visitors' Book, and the problem is finding enough time to wash the linen between guests. Our entertaining has been done in bulk, with numerous supper-parties for all ages. I am busy person doing a lot outside the home, being a magistrate, being involved with St John's Ambulance, and having various other public commitments; however, I love entertaining and have learnt to use my deep-freeze as a store cupboard.

In 1977 my husband was High Sheriff of Cornwall. This was also Jubilee Year, and we had a lovely time meeting people we would not usually have met, being entertained by Judges and local dignitaries, and entertaining them in return. The highlight was a reception on board *Britannia* when Her Majesty the Queen visited Cornwall.

In Cornwall the obligatory duties of a High Sheriff are to look after the 'Red' Judges when they come to the Crown Court at Bodmin, and to give a dinner for the ex-High Sheriffs. This last is perhaps the most important function of all, and we were determined to give them a feast to remember. Twenty-two – a record number – attended our dinner; six of them were over eighty, and three were stone deaf! On these occasions no one drives himself, lest enjoyment be inhibited, and, apart from chauffeurs and taxis, quite a few wives are to be seen waiting outside in their cars around 11.30 pm. It would be cheating if I gave you the recipes for that evening because a great friend of mine, Marika Hanbury Tenison, a professional cookery writer and a superb cook, prepared that meal for me. We had our problems, for it was in the middle of the three-day week and there was a power cut from 3.30 to 7.30 pm, but she achieved a real banquet which has never been forgotten.

I did, however, cook all the dinners for the Judges, who were fascinating people. We tried to find out beforehand what their interests were and whether there was anyone whom they would particularly like to meet, and we chose our guests very carefully to give them an enjoyable and stimulating evening. One judge finished off the evening by fetching his guitar from the car and singing calypsos to us, much to our pleasure! I did get people in to wait at table and to wash up, but I chose dishes that could be prepared ahead and would not spoil if we were a little late. I cook on electricity with two ovens, and I also have a Belling hot cupboard, so there was no problem in keeping things warm. I also had to have as much as possible done in advance so that I was free to entertain the Judge's wife during the afternoon.

I always took a lot of care over the dining-room table and the seating plan, and chose food which was not too rich and looked attractive. We had twelve guests on each occasion, but the following recipes are enough for six. They are all recipes which I have collected over the years and have altered to suit my own taste.

Pancakes stuffed with smoked salmon and crab (serves 6)

Pancakes
120g (4oz) plain flour
2 eggs
150ml (¼pt) single cream
30g (1oz) melted butter
milk
salt and pepper

Filling
30g (1oz) butter
30g (1oz) flour
300ml (½pt) warm milk
180g (6oz) smoked salmon (bits will do if available)
250g (½lb) crab
salt and pepper
1 tablespoon chopped parsley

Make the pancake batter by adding the eggs, cream and melted butter to the sifted flour and beating until smooth. Then add enough milk to make the mixture the consistency of thin cream, season, and leave to stand for 30 minutes. Melt a little butter in an omelette pan. When it is hot, add a spoonful of batter and roll the pan to coat the surface evenly. Cook over a brisk heat until brown on each side. Make enough for 6 large pancakes or 12 small ones.

Make a white sauce by melting the butter in a saucepan, adding the flour, and stirring until well blended. Add the milk, stirring all the time over a medium heat until it has thickened, and simmer gently for at least 10 minutes. Chop the smoked salmon into small pieces and add with the crab to the sauce. Season with salt and pepper, and add the parsley. Spread some of the filling on each pancake and roll up. Place them in a buttered fireproof dish. Cover with tinfoil and heat through for 30 minutes in a moderately hot oven.

These can be prepared the day before.

Beefsteak Dijonnaise (serves 6)

1kg (2lb) entrecôte steak
2 large onions
2 tablespoons olive oil
15g (½oz) butter
2 tablespoons Dijon mustard
3 tablespoons finely chopped parsley
grated rind of 2 small oranges
8 tablespoons white Cinzano
salt and freshly ground black pepper

Trim off fat and cut the steak into 6 thick slices. Peel and very thinly slice onions. Heat the olive oil in a frying pan, add steak, and brown quickly on both sides over a high heat. Lower the heat and add the butter to the oil and meat juices. Add onions and cook until lightly browned. Mix in mustard, 2 tablespoons parsley, grated rind of 1 orange and the white Cinzano, scraping the bottom of the pan with a wooden spoon. Bring the sauce to the boil, season with salt and freshly ground black pepper, and pour over the meat, spreading the onion slices evenly over the surface. Cover with tinfoil and cook in a moderate oven (190°C/375°F, gas mark 5) for 25–30 minutes until meat is tender, transfer to a heated serving dish and sprinkle over remaining orange peel and parsley.

This can also be prepared earlier in the day, and cooked in the oven just before the meal. I served it with small roast potatoes, parboiled and roasted in oil, previously heated in the oven; baby broad beans from my garden, and grilled tomatoes.

Ritz biscuit torte (serves 6)

Puddings are a problem, because some people love rich, gooey puddings while others prefer a light sorbet or fruit salad. I had a choice on this occasion of a fresh fruit salad, using raspberries, peaches and melon that I had in my deep-freeze, and the following nutty-flavoured meringue. Most of our guests had some of each.

16 Ritz biscuits
60g (2oz) chopped walnuts
30g (1oz) flaked almonds
3 egg whites
½ teaspoon baking powder
250g (8oz) castor sugar
½ teaspoon vanilla essence

Decoration
300ml (½pt) whipping cream
grated chocolate

Chop or grind the biscuits and nuts together until they look like coarse crumbs. Beat the egg whites until stiff, sift in the baking powder and sugar, and beat again until stiff. Fold in the biscuit and nut crumbs, and the vanilla. Pour into a lightly greased large ovenproof flan dish. Bake at 180°C/350°F, gas mark 4 for 40 minutes, then allow to cool. Whip the cream and spread it on top. Sprinkle with the grated chocolate, and chill for at least 3 hours before serving.

This can easily be made the day before.

The Countess of Lichfield

A Shooting Picnic

Picnics have always been an enjoyable form of eating and entertaining, from the simplest roadside cold sausage and tomato to the most elegant *fêtes champêtres* of the eighteenth and nineteenth centuries. Today we have sophisticated barbecues, with different woods to mingle with the charcoal, smart bottled sauces and pickles to baste the sizzling meat and fish, a mass of complicated and fairly useless implements which get trodden on, and many burnt fingers and helpful or otherwise suggestions from all concerned. Stone-age man with his unbutchered lump on a stick would be astonished, and at times one is still eternally grateful to the Earl of Sandwich for his inspired notion.

As children in the West of Ireland we were packed into a car, at the first glimmer of sun, to the sea where, with loaves of soda bread, marmalade and a hard-boiled egg or two, we picnicked in the brisk Atlantic breezes and made sandcastle volcanoes. Food was given low priority for, with 'growing children', quantity was the point – but even now I have a nostalgic weakness for a marmalade sandwich. We lived on an island on Lough Erne, and occasionally we would row to another island armed with an ancient blackened frying pan, some sausages, cheese and a loaf, and over a wood fire cook a fiendish mess which we called Welsh rarebit. Grey and slimy from ash and old pan and any other ingredients we fancied, it was a grim duty to the elders we had invited to tea, but we thought it was wonderful.

Even though we have cultivated a carefree indifference to the weather, I still think there is something special about eating outside, and we do it often. Some of the most enjoyable picnics have been the autumn ones when we shoot partridges, and sometimes we are lucky enough to have one of those clear golden days when we have lunch on straw bales in a stubble field beside the damson-laden hedges – when it rains we go to a barn. I am not a particularly organised picnicker in that I prefer things to look good and pretty in bowls and baskets rather than in the practical but ugly plastic box, so there is a vast amount of clutter in the back of my car, and I always have rather a nerve-racking drive to the shoot, wondering at every corner whether the Cumberland sauce has made it or if the boot is full of coleslaw. Equally there is the all-too-familiar sinking feeling of having left the bottle-opener behind, or the butter, or the plates.

I always send the guns out with a mid-morning snack of assorted alcohol, and hot sausage rolls from a baker in Nantwich – a chore to get to but worth every mile – therefore I try not to produce too stodgy a picnic, but there is always great variety. We had a wonderful cook in Ireland who used to make a melting egg-and-bacon pie for the more organised boat picnics, and this is always a great favourite.

I adore cooking, but I am lucky enough to have an extremely good cook who is a genius at translating my wild ideas, and who loves to try new things. She bakes a fine ham which we have with Cumberland sauce: it looks more festive to bring the whole thing but it is easier to slice it and pour over the sauce. Devilled chicken legs are delicious and easy to eat, and sometimes I have a good home-made game pie or terrine made from whatever is in the larder – a pigeon or an old grouse, a rabbit, pheasant, or duck. Other favourites are little brioches stuffed with smoked haddock and dill, again moderately easy to eat; and small choux pastry buns, hollowed out and filled with mousse like salmon or trout. I now rarely have a lettuce salad, as I have learned that, *if* it is eaten, it is a nightmare to cope with – too difficult to spear with a fork, and the dressing runs down the chin. But I love vegetables, and a popular (and pretty) substitute is a very finely shredded coleslaw made from red and green cabbage. On a Scottish moor I once had raw kohlrabi and swede sliced up in a dressing with chives – delicious with cold grouse. I nearly always bring baked potatoes and a jar of chives and cream, but they travel badly and lose their crispness. Venison pasties are easily transportable with enough kitchen paper around them to absorb the steam, and they are so good. Venison is a dense meat that mixes happily with all sorts of spices and tastes, and is delicious with the wild mushrooms that are abundant in the autumn woodlands.

To finish, I often have a cheesecake made with whatever is available in the garden or the hedgerows – or I have a local cheese such as blue Cheshire, or a perfect small Brie with good warm bread, plenty of fruit, homegrown apples, damsons, plums – and sloe gin or damson vodka made over previous years. But I still, after many, many picnics, nearly always forget the coffee.

Picnics can be a terrible chore, and over-complication is all too easy. A list is essential and must be made and kept – to rely on memory is taxing and risky – and transportation must be made as simple as possible. Owing to a vagary in the weather forecast, we once removed the Sunday joint from the dining-room table along with a dish of Dauphinoise potatoes, wine and one or two other small things, and rushed off to shady tree by a pond – and three of us enjoyed one of the nicest picnics we had ever eaten.

Venison pasties (serves 6)

500g (1lb) short-crust pastry
310g (10oz) cooked minced venison
1 small onion, finely chopped
salt and black pepper
½ teaspoon allspice
1 tablespoon madeira or sweet sherry
120g (4oz) finely chopped mushrooms (wild if possible)
butter
mushroom ketchup
wild rice (optional)

In a frying pan, cook the onions gently in a knob of butter until golden, add the mushrooms and madeira, and cook until soft – then add the cooked, drained, wild rice. Put the venison into the onion mixture with ½ teaspoon of mixed spice, a dash or two of mushroom ketchup, and salt and black pepper to taste. Mix it all well together and, if it seems a little dry, add a little beef stock to moisten the mixture.

Roll out the pastry to about 3mm (⅛ inch) thick and cut into rounds about 10cm (4 inches) in diameter with a cutter or anything round and suitable. Put a heap of filling onto one half of the round and fold over the other half. Damp the edges and crimp together with your fingers to seal them. Brush the pastry with a little beaten egg, prick them with a fork, and cook them on a buttered baking sheet for about 10–15 minutes in a preheated oven – 200°C/400°F, gas mark 6. Eat hot or cold or warm.

These can also be made with flaky pastry, but beware sogginess.

Miss Lamont's egg-and-bacon pie (serves 8)

370g (12oz) short crust pastry
6 hard-boiled eggs
6 rashers streaky bacon
150ml (¼pt) mornay sauce
1 large onion
15g (½oz) butter
1 beaten egg

Make the pastry and leave it in the fridge to rest. Grill the bacon until crisp and chop coarsely, slice the eggs. Chop the onion quite small, fry gently in butter until golden and drain on paper.

Cut the pastry in half and line a 23cm (9-inch) flan tin (or an enamel plate) with half the pastry and bake it blind for about 10 minutes to set. Remove it and fill it with layers beginning with onions (only on the bottom), then egg, bacon, a dribble of sauce etc until the pie is quite heaped up – pour the remaining sauce over it. Roll out the remaining pastry to make the lid, and put over the top, damping the edges and crimping them together. Make a small hole to release steam, decorate with pastry trimmings and brush with beaten egg. Cook in a preheated oven 200°C/400°F, gas mark 6 for about 15 minutes until golden. Eat hot or cold or warm.

Green and red coleslaw (makes one large bowl)

½ a red cabbage
½ a green cabbage (same size if possible)
1 coarsely grated celeriac
1 medium-sized shredded onion
2 apples, grated
2 shredded green peppers
mayonnaise
1 heaped tablespoon chopped parsley
250g (8oz) raisins (optional)

Shred the cabbages *very* finely, chop a little so that the shreds are not too long, and put in a bowl with all the other vegetables. Make a good mayonnaise with plenty of lemon juice and mustard, and bind the vegetables with this so that they are well coated. You can also add some soaked raisins if wished. Tip the mixture into a serving bowl and sprinkle with a few more raisins and quite a lot of chopped parsley.

Smoked haddock brioches (serves 12)

12 small brioches
1kg (2lb) smoked haddock
600ml (1pt) Mornay sauce, made with haddock liquid
2 heaped tablespoons chopped fresh dill (1 tablespoon dried)
white pepper

Carefully cut the tops off the brioches and gently scoop out the insides, leaving the sides approximately 6mm (¼ inch) thick. Put the brioches and lids onto a baking sheet, and bake them in a medium oven for 5 minutes or so to crisp them.

Poach the haddock in milk until just done, remove, drain, bone and flake it, reserving the liquid. Make a good Mornay sauce with some of the reserved milk and add the dill – let it infuse gently for about 5 minutes. Add enough of the sauce to the haddock to make the mixture soft but not too liquid. Pile the filling into the prepared brioches and set the lids on at an angle and serve – or put them into a suitable container well jammed together so that they do not spill.

Feeding the guns

Betty's blackberry cheesecake (serves 8–10)

250g (8oz) digestive biscuits
2 large tablespoons brown sugar
370g (12oz) good cream cheese
60g (2oz) butter (unsalted and melted)
1 beaten egg
1 teaspoon rosewater or vanilla essence
90g (3oz) castor sugar
juice of 1 lemon
blackcurrant jelly
500–750g (1–1½lb) blackberries

Put the biscuits into a food processor with the brown sugar, and dribble in the melted butter until the mixture is malleable, but not too sloppy. Press this mixture into a 46cm (18-inch) flan tin with shallow sides (or two 23cm (9-inch) cases) and cook for a few minutes in a moderate oven to crispen slightly.

Beat up the cream cheese in a bowl with the egg, sugar, rosewater (or vanilla essence if preferred) and the lemon juice until the mixture is smooth and creamy, and pour into the flan cases. Cook in a moderate oven for 15–20 minutes, or until the filling feels firm to the touch. Cool it for about 30 minutes. Arrange the blackberries on top, melt some blackcurrant jelly in a saucepan, and spoon it gently over the top of the blackberries to cover and glaze. Leave the cake to cool and set.

This is a thin cheesecake with not a vast amount of filling, so you don't get those thick wedges when cut. We have also made this with blueberries, late raspberries and *fraises des bois* which we grow in the garden, and it makes a very pretty combination of colours.

Antoinette Lucas

A Yorkshire Weekend

It seems (it is!) a long time since I set out on the extraordinary journey into the unknown that is euphemistically called marriage, and I have to admit that, in those distant days, the 'art of cooking' occupied my thoughts for almost as long as it took to say 'Galloping Gourmet'.

There seemed to be far more important things to think about – such as the 'mininess' of the latest mini – as London swung through the Sixties, and, for all I knew, looked set to swing on into the millennium.

Naturally, as a dutiful young wife, I did have a short list of a few faithful recipes, such as a wonderful way of cooking steaks in beer and a rather dangerous pudding of Mars Bars and Rice Krispies. These were terribly easy, when the accent was on *Vita* rather than *haute cuisine*, and were largely leftovers from the post-honeymoon period when some primitive instinct drove me to the kitchen and to spur-of-the-moment dinner parties.

So when the Stagnant Seventies arrived and, to my initial horror, I suddenly found myself living in North Yorkshire, I was hardly prepared for the serious business of Country Cooking. The casual, unruly dinner round the kitchen table was now a full black-tie number round monstrous mahogany tables, for which we would think nothing of driving thirty miles or so through the vilest winter weather – and staying for hours. Obviously if anybody's prepared to go to that sort of trouble they want something more than beery steak and Mars Bars.

Initially, my attempts to rise to the occasion were only partially successful; the food was fine, but I seemed to spend most of the day and the night in the kitchen – which seemed to be an over-reaction. I rapidly came to the conclusion that I should stick to

recipes that did not demand my constant attention. Since then the compromise of good food and freedom has come to represent the 'art of cooking' for me, though there does seem to be a certain Parkinson side-effect which suggests that the number of dinner-parties we have expands in relation to the refinement of this particular approach.

Of course, my initial dread of spending the rest of my days in spectacular isolation in North Yorkshire now seems absurd, as we seem to have become a handy staging post for anybody on their way to or from Scotland in the winter, while the summer months are busy with a multifarious and fascinating flow of visitors (mostly from America) who seem to prefer staying in a private house rather than a hotel while visiting 'The Old Country'.

I became a hostess for Old Country Tours of Boston, Mass, some time ago now, but I shall never forget my first season of 'guests who pay'. The Smirnoffs were due to arrive in June and a brief note of introduction from Boston was some help. I learned that H.O. Smirnoff owned a number of restaurants in Duluth, was sixty-eight years old, married to May, with a daughter called Rose who played the violin, though not, I hoped, under this roof. Their interests were listed as horse-racing, fishing and opera, and they were to stay for three days. I applied myself to the problems of stimulating a restaurateur's palate, and my initial reaction was to push the sauce boat out with good Old Country fare. Grouse rose in my mind, and settled again as a small voice suggested that one should never give grouse to complete strangers from Duluth. Perhaps blinis and stroganoff would be more suitable, but it would take a better, and braver, cook than me to go Russian with a restaurateur called Smirnoff. So what to do? What would titillate, surprise and amuse a fishing, racing opera buff? The answer had to be Chinese Seafood Rolls with Sweet and Sour Sauce. What else could mix the subtle flavours of a day at the races with a dash of the exotica of opera? If my Seafood Rolls didn't surprise them, then nothing would, and within minutes I had my beansprouts sprouting on a flannel inside a plastic bag in the airing cupboard.

Safe with this ace up my sleeve, I awaited the Smirnoffs with equanimity, and ran to the front door when the bell rang that rainy afternoon. I opened the door, and froze. Ho Smirnoff and family were Chinese, and Rose was clutching her violin.

My next guests were the Gradys from Dallas who positively glittered with diamonds and arrived in one of those larger American station-wagons which have been as common as dinosaurs since the first oil crisis. Everything I had assumed about Texans, after a lifetime of cowboy films and Dallas, smacked of understatement. Jim Grady stood six-foot-four in his stockinged feet, which meant that with his hat and boots he was out of this world. Apart from the inevitable steak breakfasts consumed during the four days they were with us, the greatest compliments were paid to my Medallions of Pork with Orange and Ginger. My final guests that summer were three ladies, a Doctor McInnes, otherwise known as Merlin, and her two companions, Guinevere and Igraine, from the Cincinnati Round Table. In their honour I created a pudding which has been known to this day as Caprice Camelot.

Chinese seafood rolls (serves 6)

Filling
1 tablespoon grated carrot
1 tablespoon finely chopped celery
1 tablespoon finely chopped spring onion
55g (2oz) drained beansprouts
110g (4oz) cooked flaked haddock
110g (4oz) peeled prawns
2 teaspoons oil
1 teaspoon castor sugar
freshly ground black pepper

Batter
5fl oz water
½ teaspoon salt
55g (2oz) plain flour
2 eggs

Beat the eggs together and reserve 2 tablespoons of beaten egg for later use. Beat the water, salt and flour into the remaining beaten egg until smooth.

Use the batter to make 12 thin pancakes of approximately 15cm (6 inches) in diameter.

Blanch the carrot and celery together in boiling water for 2 minutes, then drain and mix with remaining filling ingredients.

Divide the mixture between the pancakes and roll them, folding in the sides and using the reserved beaten egg to seal the edges.

To freeze. Pack rolls in a rigid container, cover and freeze.

To serve. While still frozen, deep fry the rolls in hot oil for 5–7 minutes, until crisp and golden. Serve with the sweet and sour sauce.

Sweet and sour sauce
1 tablespoon oil
1 onion, peeled and diced
142ml (¼pt) dry white wine
1 tablespoon wine vinegar
1 tablespoon peach chutney
1 tablespoon tomato ketchup
1 tablespoon soy sauce
1 tablespoon mustard
salt
freshly ground black pepper
pinch of mixed spice
pinch of chilli powder
1 tablespoon cornflour
6 tablespoons water

Heat the oil in a pan and gently fry the onion until soft and transparent. Pour in the wine. Increase the heat and boil for 2 minutes. Add vinegar, chutney, tomato ketchup, soy sauce, mustard, salt, pepper, mixed spice and chilli powder. Cover and simmer for 20 minutes. Cool slightly, then sieve or blend in a liquidiser and return to the pan. Blend the cornflour with the water and stir into the sauce. Bring back to the boil and simmer for 2–3 minutes.

Salmon en croûte (serves 6)

1.25kg (2½lb) salmon
85g (3oz) butter
chopped ginger
1 tablespoon raisins
salt and pepper
short crust pastry

Skin and bone the salmon so that there are two flat pieces. Put the butter and the raisins and chopped ginger in a Magimix or other food processor.

Spread ⅔ of the mixture in between the salmon and put the rest on the top of the salmon.

Roll out the pastry and join it underneath the salmon. Place on foil, decorate and brush with beaten egg and cream. Bake for 30 minutes at 220°C/425°F, gas mark 7.

Sauce
2 shallots
1 teaspoon flour
300ml (½pt) cream
1 teaspoon Dijon mustard
2 egg yolks, and 2 tablespoons cream
chopped tarragon, parsley and chervil
1 lemon

Sweat shallots in butter with chopped tarragon, parsley and chervil. Stir in flour. Add ½pt cream. Salt and pepper and mustard. Cook gently for 10 minutes. Beat in egg yolks and cream. Thicken without boiling. Add lemon juice to taste.

Pastry
120g (4oz) margarine
120g (4oz) lard
225g (8oz) flour
salt and pepper

Medallions of pork with orange and ginger
(serves 6)

2 pork tenderloins
2 oranges
55g (2oz) butter
30g (1oz) thinly sliced preserved ginger
1 tablespoon syrup from preserved ginger
4 tablespoons wine vinegar
salt and pepper
110g (4oz) soft brown sugar
1 tablespoon cornflour
142ml (¼pt) chicken stock

To serve
1 orange, peeled and sliced

Cut the tenderloins into 2.5cm (1-inch) thick slices and beat until a 6mm (¼ inch) thick. Remove rind from half an orange and cut into very thin strips. Squeeze the juice from both oranges and set aside.

Melt the butter in a frying pan, fry the pork on both sides until lightly browned. Remove the pork and arrange in a serving dish.

Mix together the orange juice, brown sugar, ginger syrup, cornflour, vinegar, stock, salt and pepper, and pour into the pan. Bring mixture to the boil, then cover and simmer for 5–6 minutes. Stir in the sliced ginger and orange-rind strips and simmer for a further 2–3 minutes. Pour the sauce over the meat.

Caprice Camelot (serves 6)

Cake
2 tablespoons toasted almonds, coarsely chopped
110g (4oz) castor sugar
4 eggs
110g (4oz) flour
30g (1oz) unsweetened cocoa powder
110g (4oz) butter, melted and cooled

Syrup
4 tablespoons Jamaican rum
4 tablespoons syrup from chestnuts

Crème Chantilly
275g (10 oz) thick cream
2 tablespoons castor sugar
2 tablespoons iced water
few drops of vanilla essence
4 glacé chestnuts, coarsely chopped

Garnish
110g (4oz) chocolate in small pieces
6/8 glacé chestnuts, drained

Heat the oven to 200°C/400°F, gas mark 6. Prepare 20cm (8-inch) ring mould by buttering it well and then sprinkling the almonds inside.

Beat the sugar and eggs until light and fluffy. Sift the flour and the cocoa powder together and gently fold into the egg mixture, using a metal spoon. Fold in the cooled, melted butter.

Pour the mixture into the mould. Bake for 25–30 minutes or until the cake shrinks slightly from the sides of the mould. Remove from the oven and turn out, after 5 minutes, onto a wire rack to cool.

Split the cold cake horizontally in two. Moisten the two cut sides with the rum and an equal quantity of syrup from the chestnuts. Spread with the Crème Chantilly. Sandwich the cake together.

Melt the chocolate in a bowl over hot water, then carefully spoon the melted chocolate over the cake. Surround with whole glacé chestnuts for serving.

Crème Chantilly
Whip the cream with the sugar until stiff. Add the iced water and vanilla essence and whip again until the cream is soft and fluffy. Fold in the coarsely chopped glacé chestnuts and chill.

Sarah Lucas

Cooking for Christmas

I sometimes feel I spend my whole life 'getting ahead'. Other farmers' wives with school-age children must know exactly what I mean: life seems to consist of a series of never-ending meals, and it is often difficult to drum up fresh enthusiasm and imagination about each and every one.

So I plan and cook for Christmas in November, setting aside a special starred week when *nobody* is allowed to interrupt, thus knowing that there will then be little chance of being caught out by a sudden deluge of unexpected friends and relations. It is also in my own interests since my family sweetly don't allow me inside the kitchen on my birthday, which happens to fall two days before Christmas. My organisational skills were not up to what happened on one fateful occasion. The butcher delivered the turkey, and when we returned from my birthday lunch we found that my daughter's cat had made short work of one of the legs. There is not a lot you can do at 5 pm on 23 December with your entire complement of 'in-laws' coming on Christmas Day. The turkey was washed, cooked and carved, limbless side to the wall, and no one was any the wiser!

I do not usually freeze dishes and do not like the idea of eating ready-cooked food; however, with the amount of people we have staying and passing through the house over the Christmas to New Year period, I have to swallow my pride. There are various well-tried and favourite dishes that freeze beautifully, such as *profiteroles au chocolat*, which can be frozen with the cream or *crème pâtissière* already inside. Fresh

Finishing touches

fruit sorbets, using any fruit you like, work well – our favourites are red and black currant – as do ice creams; pâtés and savoury mousses such as haddock or smoked salmon are all well-tried, and it is a tremendous relief to feel that I have some reliable old friends standing by for such busy times. A good stock of frozen prawns, scallops and crabmeat is useful and quickly made up into any number of delicious first courses. We buy most of our fish from Port Isaac in Cornwall, where we also farm. We grow and freeze a certain amount of fruit and vegetables – what could be nicer than a dish of tiny french beans or a redcurrant and gooseberry pie in mid-winter?

Two other standbys that keep their good looks and taste when frozen are my blackcurrant bombe, and a chocolate roulade which freezes, icing sugar and all, but needs extra care at the wrapping stage, and doesn't benefit from being squashed! I do not, however, freeze mince pies. They keep beautifully in cake tins, not that they are allowed to keep anywhere for long.

Certain things like the Christmas cake actually benefit from being made in advance. I try to make mine in October so that it has plenty of time to mature. It is a lovely recipe given to me when first married and is always highly appreciated by the hordes of ravenous teenage boys who descend on us at Christmas – more so than by my three-year-old daughter, who can't understand why I won't pick the currants out for her!

On Christmas Eve I am left free to perform the ritual I enjoy most. I gather together all the bits and pieces searched for at odd times throughout the year, and attempt to transform the dining-room into a setting which does justice to the season and, of course, to all my cooking!

Smoked salmon pâté (serves 4–6)

250g (8oz) smoked salmon bits
180g (6oz) butter
150g (5oz) double cream
lemon juice
paprika
salt and pepper

Melt butter. Chop smoked salmon bits and put into Magimix or liquidiser, pour in melted butter in a thin stream and process until smooth, season and cool. Whip cream and fold into salmon mixture with lemon juice to taste. Turn into pot. Chill (or freeze). Serve with toast fingers or fresh bread.

My perfect turkey

(bearing in mind there are many 'expert' theories on how to cook this often over-cooked bird.)

Take an 11kg (22lb) dressed and stuffed, fresh, hen bird. Smear the entire bird with a generous amount of fairly soft butter. Place *breast down* in roasting tin in top right oven of Aga (approx. 190°–200°C/375°–400°F, gas mark 6) for about 2 hours. Turn the bird over and move down to bottom right oven 150°C/300°F, gas mark 2) for a further 1¼ hours. Dish onto serving dish (I do this at about 11.45 am before my guests are due) and transfer the turkey to the bottom left-hand oven.

Make the gravy and get the worst of the pans washed up by 12 noon when, with luck, your guests will promptly arrive to find you ready to open the Christmas Day champagne with only the vegetables left to do. Meanwhile the turkey will very gently go on cooking for a further hour or two and, when carved, will be moist and succulent and not the poor dried bird you so often come across.

If you don't have an Aga, continue cooking at 150°C/300°F, gas mark 2 for a further 1½ hours, then dish onto a serving dish, cover with foil (so that no heat can escape) and a drying-up cloth over the foil, and leave to stand for 30 minutes before carving.

Chocolate roulade (serves 6)

180g (6oz) Menier chocolate
5 eggs (separated)
180g (6oz) castor sugar
3 tablespoons hot water
icing sugar
300ml (½pt) double cream

Prepare large shallow tin 34.3cm × 24cm (13½ inches × 9½ inches), brush with oil and line with greaseproof or bakewell paper.

Break chocolate into pieces into a small basin, and place over a pan of hot water to melt. Stir from time to time. When completely melted, add 3 tablespoons of hot water (taken from pan), mix in well.

Beat together the castor sugar and egg yolks until pale in colour, and then add melted chocolate mixture, beat well.

Whisk the egg whites until stiff and fold into the chocolate mixture. Pour into baking tin and spread evenly. Place in middle of a moderate oven (180°C/350°F, gas mark 4) and bake for 15–20 minutes. Remove from oven, cover with a sheet of greaseproof paper and a damp cloth, and leave overnight.

Turn roulade onto a sheet of greaseproof paper that has been generously dusted with icing sugar. Peel away the baking paper. Lightly whip the cream (it can be flavoured if you wish) and spread over the roulade. Roll up like a swiss roll, using the sugared paper to help.

Put onto a serving plate and, if you are to freeze it at this stage, wrap carefully with clingfilm. Put into a freezing bag and seal tightly. Freeze at once. This freezes beautifully, but do be careful not to put anything on top of it while it is in the freezer or it will surely squash!

Raspberry or redcurrant sorbet (serves 6–8)

500g (1lb) frozen raspberries or redcurrants
180g (6oz) sugar
juice of 1 large lemon
2 egg whites

Place the fruit and sugar together in the Magimix or liquidiser and purée, add lemon juice and a few teaspoons of rosewater (if you have any). Whisk the egg whites until stiff. Fold purée into the egg whites. Turn into a plastic container (or glass bowl) and freeze. This, when spooned into small glasses and served with langues du chat biscuits, looks a pretty colour and has a cool, fresh taste.

Blackcurrant bombe (serves 8)

300ml (½pt) double cream
1 tablespoon castor sugar

Whip cream and sugar together until stiff. Spread over the inside of a 900ml (1½pt) pudding basin. Put to freeze.

250g (½lb) frozen blackcurrants
5 tablespoons water
15g (½oz) powdered gelatine
120g (4oz) castor sugar
300ml (½pt) double cream
2 egg whites

Put the blackcurrants into a pan with half the water. Cover and set on a low heat, to soften. Put remaining water into a small bowl and sprinkle gelatine over. Allow to stand for a few minutes. Remove blackcurrants from heat and add the sugar. Stir and add the soaked gelatine, the heat of the pan will melt the gelatine, continue mixing until the gelatine is fully dissolved. Purée this mixture, and leave to cool. Lightly whip the cream and beat the egg whites until stiff. Fold gently into the blackcurrant mixture. Turn complete mixture into the, by now, frozen cream-lined basin and freeze again. Wrap carefully before storing in the freezer.

Cake

1kg (2lb) currants
500g (1lb) sultanas
500g (1lb) raisins
250g (½lb) glacé cherries
250g (½lb) mixed peel
175g (6oz) shredded almonds
grated rind 1 lemon
500g (1lb) butter
500g (1lb) Barbados sugar (dark)
560g (18oz) plain flour
1 level teaspoon salt
2 level teaspoons baking powder
9 eggs
3 tablespoons brandy

This quantity is for a 25.4cm (10-inch) square tin or 2 × 19cm (7½-inch) or 20cm (8-inch) round tins.

Prepare the tin. Melt a little lard and brush the inside of the tin, line tin with double greaseproof paper to about 7.5cm (3 inches) above tin. Brush with melted lard. Put a width of brown paper around outside of tin. Stand tin on baking sheet covered with ¼ inch of salt to prevent burning.

Smoked salmon pâté

Heat oven at 150°C/300°F, gas mark 2.
Prepare fruit. Wash and dry if necessary. Halve cherries. Chop peel. Shred almonds if necessary. Mix all fruit, peel etc together.

Beat butter and sugar until light and fluffy. Add lemon rind.

Weigh flour and add the salt. Divide into three equal parts. Add one part to the fruit. Mix thoroughly, and add one part to the baking powder and mix well.

Add the well-beaten eggs a little at a time to the butter and sugar mixture, beating thoroughly. Add a little of the remaining one third of the flour alternately with the egg, beating well.

Stir in (not beat) the flour and baking powder. When mixed thoroughly add the floured fruit. Stir well. Add the brandy.

The mixture should be a fairly stiff consistency.

Press well into tin and bake below middle of oven for 2–3 hours. Do not look for $1\frac{1}{2}$ hours, then reduce oven temperature to 140°C/275°F, gas mark 1 and look every half hour or so. When closing oven door, ensure you do this gently. Cake should be cooked for $2\frac{1}{2}$ hours but depends on cooker. Test with skewer.

When ready, remove cake. Let it stand for 30 minutes before turning out of tin, and leave for a few hours or one night. Then wrap in two sheets greaseproof paper and put in a good tin.

If possible, make about eight weeks before using, but if slightly under-done, it is very good one to two weeks after baking.

Lady Lymington

A London Buffet

For purposes of self-respect it is necessary to assume that the *entire* point of all entertaining is to give your guests the very best time possible, the limits being imposed only by your resources, both financial and technical, and never, ever, by laziness. The first thing to do, then, is to survey these resources with all frankness.

In the old days, when I entertained in the country, this meant calculating the largest number of people who could eat indoors supposing the weather were inclement. To my surprise, this only happened once and a jolly time was had by all, perching on furniture and dribbling mayonnaise into each other's shoes. Everyone was very sporting, but I think the English quite like a disaster so long as it is not too awful!

As the buffet-at-home was so popular in the country, I have transported the idea to London, where it is very much 'business as usual'. It now takes place in what I think of as my garden, since I work on it harder than I ever did on the country acres, but it could more accurately be described as a yard. The principles are just the same, only the quantity and range of dishes are different.

Getting the drinks department to work smoothly is essential, and means unfailing

'Exuberant profusion'

buckets of ice and iced lemonade for the Pimm's, and a fleet-footed backer-up for speedy delivery to guests too shy to seize for themselves. Pimm's is always the runaway favourite, with white wine second. I always have a selection of other drinks too, as there is often someone who has been told to drink whisky by the doctor, sometimes, indeed, all through meals. Who are these doctors? Where are they? Mine never says anything like that!

I count on the sight of the table eliciting exclamations of extreme greed, an essential part of the cook's gratification. Although the recipes in themselves are not complicated, they have been chosen with a view to providing a varied and rolling panorama of gastronomic delight. The golden quiches, the tomatoes, the green beans, the dark aubergines, the pale jugs of mayonnaise and so on should be artfully arranged to form some sort of pattern giving the maximum contrast. The most dispiriting sight is a buffet where everything is chopped and covered with bottled mayonnaise disconsolately leaking water at the edges. The very best dishes to use are all the peculiar ones that do not match: earthenware for the potato salad, white to display the kidney beans, something flowery on which the stuffed eggs can sit. In this way an impression of accidental and exuberant profusion is achieved which is far more enticing than rows of matched anything, which quickly looks like more or less grand hotel-ware, carrying with it the dreaded stigma that The Caterers Have Been Here.

A note on table-laying: never be tempted to gild the lily by adding flowers of any kind to the table out of doors. The poor things look terrible next to their growing brethren.

Many years ago my business partner said to me that my salads wouldn't be so disgusting if only I would stop putting lettuce in them. This remark struck home deeply, for at that time I was still very much a lettuce-and-tomato lady. Strenuous efforts were made to improve, which finally resulted in a certain amount of blood to the head and, in my turn, rather to my horror, I heard myself remark that anyone who served less than seven salads was a slob. As a result of this *bêtise* I have had to make rather a lot of salads!

The English have been accused of being long on decoration and short on content in the kitchen, the favourite jibe being: two minutes to pour the packet custard onto the bought sponge and bought jam, call it a trifle, then spend an hour with the angelica and tweezers putting daisies on top. While I greatly disapprove of this way of carrying on, there is no doubt that at least a certain neatness does add to the appeal of a buffet. The beans should all point the same way, the tomato salad should have lines of little basil leaves running across it, alternate stuffed eggs can be trimmed with paprika and green olive halves making a checked effect, and I sometimes put the date, in a circle, in slivers of black olives on a pizza. The one thing to remember is not to use the same extras on two dishes, thus exposing a poverty of invention.

The recipes that follow are the only ones that are complicated enough for an explanation; otherwise, as I have said before, even the simplest salads should be treated with visible respect. Even the humble beetroot can be dressed up to look like a garnet if you use only the really small ones, and roll them in olive oil after skinning.

Brawn

I first made this at the behest of my husband, who was lamenting its demise, and it now has a small but keen fan club, mainly composed of elderly gentlemen who become very nostalgic about their childhoods. It is a great deal of trouble to make and hardly for the squeamish, but those who do like it, like it very much indeed. One point in its favour is that it freezes splendidly. I usually make it straight into 1½pt tupperware containers: this recipe makes four or five.

1 large pig's head (get the butcher to quarter it for you).
1kg (2lb) leg beef, cut in 4
2 carrots
2 sticks of celery
2 onions
herbs
salt and pepper
powdered cloves★
nutmeg★
pistachio nuts (optional)

★It is very difficult to give a quantity. Start with a saltspoon of cloves and half a saltspoon of nutmeg and adjust to taste *after* the liquid has been reduced.

Clean the head well and leave in salted water for about 3 hours. Put all the ingredients into an enormous saucepan and bring to simmering point, simmer for 3 hours, then see if flesh falls away from the bone really easily. If not, carry on simmering. When ready, take out the head and meat. Throw away the vegetables. Remove all flesh from the head, return bones to stock, and boil fast to reduce until the stock sets to form a very firm jelly. Test by putting some on a saucer which can be cooled in the fridge.

While liquid is reducing, chop the meat from the head finely, also the beef, but take care not to mash it as it should be very tender now. Apportion the meat into the chosen dishes. When the stock is ready, skim off fat and strain. Finally, pour over meat in moulds until all meat is covered, and leave to set.

Stuffed aubergines (serves 16)

8 small aubergines
4 medium onions
300ml (½pt) olive oil
1 tablespoon sugar
1 lemon
2 × 397g (14oz) tins of tomatoes
300ml (½pt) fine bread crumbs
15 cloves of garlic
parsley
salt

Halve the aubergines and cover with salt. Leave to stand for 1½ hours. Wash. Scoop out interior of aubergines, leaving shell about the thickness of grapefruit peel. Put onions and aubergine pith through the grater of mixing machine with garlic and parsley, or chop finely. Add tinned tomatoes and stir well to break up tomatoes. Add salt and sugar. Pile this mixture into aubergine shells and sprinkle breadcrumbs over the top. Squeeze lemon over breadcrumbs. Pour oil very carefully over the breadcrumbs so as not to knock them off. Put about 300ml (½pt) of water in the bottom of the baking dish and put in the oven at 180°C/350°F, gas mark 4 for 45–50 minutes. The aubergine shell should feel really soft to the point of the knife.

When they are cooked, baste lightly with the remains of the liquid in which they have cooled. Then, when they have absorbed their full, remove to dry dish, so that while being as moist as possible they are not actually wet.

Pizza

This mixture is very adaptable, and the pizzas can be made in tins of varying shapes and sizes, according to resources. The quantities given are for four 20cm or 23cm (8 or 9 inch) pizzas. I usually make four or eight as it is very little more trouble and they freeze perfectly and make ideal emergency food, with no accompaniments needed.

Dough
500g (1lb) strong flour (Marriage's)
1 desertspoon sugar
150ml (¼pt) warm milk
1 teaspoon salt
30g (1oz) fresh yeast
4 eggs
120g (4oz) well-softened butter

Add crumbled yeast and sugar to well-warmed milk and leave until yeast is working well. Put salt in flour in a large basin and stand in a warm place. Beat eggs. When yeast mixture is working nicely add to the eggs. Add this liquid to the dry mixture and stir well before adding the soft butter. Beat well. Cover with a cloth wrung out in hot water and leave to double in bulk – about 50 minutes. A corner of an Aga, a Belling warming cabinet, the linen cupboard, somewhere really warm gets the dough moving quicker. During this time prepare the ingredients for the tops. All these quantities can be varied according to individual taste as long as the over-all amount remains about the same. When making a quantity of pizzas it is not a bad idea to vary the tops for the sake of both appearance and flavour.

Basic
370g (12oz) onions (unpeeled weight)
1 × 150g (5oz) can tomato purée
1 × 397g (14oz) can tinned tomatoes
flat dessertspoon dried herbs, basil, marjoram, oregano or mix.

Fry onions till transparent, not limp, add tinned tomatoes and paste. Salt and pepper. Stir well to break up any large tomatoes.

Extras
250g (½lb) lightly fried, sliced mushrooms
tinned anchovy fillets (split)
250g (½lb) cheese cut into fat matchsticks (preferably mozzarella)
120g (¼lb) black olives, stoned and quartered
120g (¼lb) lean chopped ham or fried bacon

When the dough is well-risen, turn it onto a very well-floured board, and also flour your hands. Cut it into four and put a piece into each of the greased tins. Pull the dough quickly and lightly till it corresponds to the shape of the tin. Do not overwork it. It need not be of uniform thickness; should a hole appear, it can easily be remedied by pinching off a little bit from a thicker section and just putting it over the hole.

Next, spoon the tomato mixture generously over the pizzas taking it almost up to the very edge. Then arrange your extras as fast as you can in the manner of your choice. In general I would not go heavy on the anchovies and the olives on the same pizza as these are the stronger-flavoured of the trimmings. For decoration, rings and ray patterns are both attractive, but the smell of the things is the most attractive of all, so do not spend too long on this as the pizzas must be left in the warm to rise for a further 15 minutes before going into a pre-heated oven (230°C/450°F, gas mark 8). They will be cooked in about 20 minutes; test by putting the point of a knife into the part without topping at the edge. If it comes out clean, the pizzas are done. If they are for immediate consumption, I let the outer rims turn really golden. If they are for freezing and re-heating, I take them out when they are just done and pale gold in colour.

Cecilia McEwen

A Hogmanay Breakfast

In stark contrast to the more elegant Christmases and New Years of my youth, the shock of the Scottish New Year was a monumental body blow: grey skies, no festive parties, and the sole objective appearing to be the achievement of complete inebriation and leglessness before dawn and continuing well into the following year.

The mornings after the Eve in Austria were spent 'skiing it off', or, for the older and frailer (for whatever reason), a gentle morning's recuperation in a *Konditorei* was the habit. Starting with black coffee and iced water, followed by *geschpritzen* – white wine and soda; helped on by a *goulasch-suppe* and sharpened by schnapps – and then begin again at the beginning.

The unhappy contrast of trying to host a conventional weekend party at New Year in Scotland, sometimes lasting up to five or six days, depending on the day of the week it falls, was a damp squib: no one around to help, most of the guests in pubs as the soufflé hit the table, in every sense of the word, the house in increasing stages of disarray, and well-prepared food polished off as if by the Pied Piper's rats every night; ham hacked to something resembling the steppes, smoked turkey a shining skeleton, and the breakfast eggs vanished, except for the pile of plates and saucepans egg-clogged in the sink. The wonder of the non-stick pan remains uncharted.

Now, with age and a quicker temper, the New Year has taken on a military discipline. A hard core of regulars, prepared to put up with the inconvenience, books in early to avoid disappointment, appears on time for dinner, plumps up the occasional cushion and is tactfully appreciative of the volatile hostess.

110 CECILIA McEWEN

'The volatile hostess'

On New Year's Day, the first shattered guest totters down early, wearing his motoring cap. The worse the hangover, the earlier the riser. Even by this ungodly hour, teeth clenched and eyes glazed, it is essential to have the basic spread ready. The eggs, provided there are any left, have to be made to order, as by 12.15 they resemble mangled frisbees. Strong black Italian coffee, China tea, fresh grapefruit juice, kedgeree, fishcakes, piles of very crisp streaky bacon, grilled sausages, fried black pudding, Sophie McEwen's home-made bread, home-made marmalade, strawberry and raspberry jam, local honey (not ours – I may yet get into my bee-keeping outfit) and the usual parade of bottled sauces the British are so addicted to, are all laid on.

Confronted by this restorative feast to prepare the guests for further 'first-footing' and pub-crawling, my morning's prayer is – may this be the last!

Kedgeree (serves 4)

3 smoked haddock fillets
120g (4oz) salmon
1 medium onion, sliced
4 heaped tablespoons of rice
scant teaspoon of curry powder
2 hard-boiled eggs
parsley
salt and pepper
butter
cream

Pour boiling water over the haddock. Allow 3 minutes before draining, removing the skin, and chopping roughly.

Fry the onion in olive oil until golden, stir in the curry powder and the rice, and pour in 600ml (1pt) of water. Boil gently for 10 minutes. Add the haddock and salmon, and continue to cook for 10 minutes until the liquid is gone. Season to taste, add chopped eggs and parsley, some knobs of butter and a splash of cream, and, if kept on a hotplate, an egg yolk or two to stop it drying out.

Sophie McEwen's Bread (2 large loaves)

Just a word or two about bread: due to the nature of yeast (provided it isn't too old or exposed to air for too long), bread cannot fail to rise, sooner or later. It is quite untrue that bread is difficult to make.

1.4kg (3lb) spring wheat flour
900g (2lb) strong white (plain) flour
12g ($\frac{1}{2}$oz) dried yeast
37g ($1\frac{1}{2}$oz) salt
50g (2oz) butter or margarine
600–900ml (1–$1\frac{1}{2}$pt) warm water

Use non-stick tins or baking trays

Put the yeast in a small bowl and pour enough warm water to cover it, leave till it goes frothy (about 15 minutes). Melt butter slowly. Mix flour and salt together in a large bowl. Rub the melted butter into the flour and add the yeast – which should be creamy, without lumps – rubbing this into the mixture. Start adding the water – not too much at once – and knead it into the mixture. Go on adding water until the mixture binds – it shouldn't be sticky, and if it is, add a little more flour. Knead the dough (squashing and punching it with your hands) until it has a springy resistant consistency.

Put the bowl with the mixture in it inside a plastic carrier bag (which keeps it moist) in a fairly warm room and leave it to rise. This should take 2–3 hours, but don't panic if it takes longer. Just leave the dough and don't add anything, the yeast has been activated by the water, salt and warmth and has got to make the dough rise. Leave it overnight if necessary. When the mixture rises it is very puffy and at least twice its original size.

Put enough dough in the tins to half-fill them and leave it to rise again. This second 'proving' shouldn't take long and the dough will rise to the top of the tins. Pre-heat the oven for 10–15 minutes at 230°C/450°F, gas mark 8 and bake the bread for about 40 minutes, turning the tins to let them brown evenly. The best way to check that the bread is ready is to take the loaf out of the tin and tap the bottom. It should make a dull, hollow thump.

NB The amount of water used and the time spent on kneading depends on the flour – remember that the mixture shouldn't be too sticky, more springy. This bread does not seem to mind deep-freezing! It sometimes even improves.

Lady Maclean

Perfectly Simple Cooking

'*Faites simple*'; the words of the great Escoffier should be above every kitchen stove.

Though I don't think anything can match the slow, steady *coin du feu* heat of a solid fuel cooker, there are times when one wants something more spirited, so a four-burner, bottled-gas auxiliary with a good grill has been installed on one side of my Aga, and an excellent Creda electric oven (bought for £50 at a local sale) on the other.

I know that for everyday eating in our family one large, satisfying main course is enough, and although it is usually preceded by an appetiser and rounded off by cheese and salad and fruit, these are mere contrivances. So now (may the good Lord be praised) there is only one dish to work on and worry about. That dish can be as simple as I like, traditionally regional, exotically foreign, or it can come straight out of the top of my head.

In the past I have fantasised happily about the conversion of our large, old-fashioned, and largely undecorated kitchen into the ultimate of practical, labour-saving, modern elegance, but in the end I have not done much to change it. We eat off the old scrubbed-pine kitchen table covered with a faded Indian or sprigged cotton tablecloth.

A locally made cook's table stands in front of my Aga. It is rectangular and one can work from any side of it. It has a butcher's block top with a removable, let-in 'dry sink' which is very useful for collecting dry or wet mess. The knives and spoons stand in two wooden boxes in the middle, there are deep shelves with crocks and containers below, and sieves and gadgets hang on hooks from the sides.

Some of the finest ingredients in the world can be found on our doorstep: famous Loch Fyne herring (and kippers); fresh oysters; mackerel; sea trout; salmon; scallops; clams; 'Norway' prawns; haunches of venison; saddles of roe-deer; farm-yard chickens; hill lamb; shorthorn beef; heather honey and strawberries. (My French governess, who taught me to cook, always crossed herself with the first June strawberry

before popping it into her mouth, and I was never certain whether her ensuing expression of beatitude was caused by Grace or greed.) Fat raspberries, mountain blackberries, gulls' eggs, wood chanterelles, are all available without going anywhere near a shop, which is lucky because the nearest grocer is twenty miles away.

This year I have edged my way towards a watershed, and my Highland hospitality will suffer a sea-change. I have closed the doors of our beautiful dining-room. From now on a hill-farmer's kitchen is to be the setting for a new kind of entertaining and a new style of eating. It will be adaptable and informal, 'laid back', I believe it is called in America. Sumptuous simplicity at its best: a ploughman's lunch of home-made bread and cheese and pickles when I am feeling tired. . . ? Well, just possibly.

I have studied the life-style of our own younger generation and have always been astonished how well my children cope the moment they leave the nest and start making one of their own. The child that could not boil an egg, and had to have the top of it sliced off for her before she would eat it, becomes overnight the capable housewife who entertains multitudes with delicious food and perfect confidence.

How do they do it? They cut out pretentiousness and formality and concentrate on good company and good food. Their food is genuine, fresh, countrified; it does not always look terrific but it always tastes delicious. They are not frightened of machines. They accept amateur help and they chatter while they work – or listen to 'mind-blowing' music. They can do two things at once – well. They are not, like me, tradition's slave. They manipulate it. They never get bogged down in detail and, when things go wrong, they bluff their way through. And amazingly, the result has style, albeit a new and different style; more comfortable and comforting, more relaxed, like nursery teas, or farmhouse cooking at its best. And, of course, they are right: I have eaten good food all over the world but the meals that stand out in my memory are, for the most part, perfectly simple ones.

I once ate a remarkable meal in the garden of His Magnificence, the Rector of Marburg University in Germany. It consisted solely of his own very first new potatoes dug from the garden that morning and served with home-made herb-flavoured cream cheese and the best chilled white wine from the Palatinate I have ever drunk. And I have eaten steamed baby courgettes with melted butter and Parmesan in a villa on the Bosporus; a niece's grilled sausages on a bed of perfectly cooked lentils; a clam chowder made from our local, hand-dug clams, to an American submariner's recipe; a wonderful fricassee of rabbit and wild mushrooms and herbs that I ate among almond blossom in the Roman ruins of Cervi; a strange and exquisite Chinese boeuf stroganov in the dining-car of the Ulan Bator-Peking express; a tender lamb kebab (marinated in olive oil and local lemons) on a pale-green Turkish purée of aubergines at Eskişehir; the perfect Yorkshire hot-pot in a very old pub in Richmond; my first *poulet de Bresse* as a Sunday treat in a village near Beaune; and a Virginian comforter called Brunswick Stew which should be made of squirrel, but, thank goodness, wasn't. And from our own barn-side? Chanterelles that we cooked in a little butter and cream and poured over green noodles – a dish, like the others, of rare and sumptuous simplicity.

Poaching your own

How I boil my local salmon and sea trout

The mystery of this method is that it works equally well with small or large fish.

Put your cleaned and scraped whole fish into cold water in a fish kettle. It should cover the fish by two or three fingers. Bring the water gently to the boil and boil briskly for exactly 2 minutes. Then take the fish kettle off the fire and lift out the strainer and fish, balancing them sideways over the kettle so that the fish cools in the steam.

We eat it hot with steamed cucumber chunks filled with peeled green grapes and a large sauce-boat of Hollandaise sauce, or cold with a *sauce verte* of my own device – a 2-yolk mayonnaise, unsharpened by vinegar or lemon juice, but with half a cup of whipped cream and 2 tablespoons of sorrel purée folded in before serving.

If you cook salmon this way it will always be perfectly juicy and firm – and never over-cooked.

Pasticada Korculanska (serves 6–8)

A Yugoslavian recipe. Braised beef, stuffed with bacon and garlic and cooked in a tomato sauce with *Prosek* (see ingredients) and prunes, served in its own rich sauce with an accompaniment of home-made potato gnocchi, or noodles, if you prefer them.

1½kg (3lb) slice of best topside, without fat 7.5–10cm (3–4 inches thick)
small bottle good wine vinegar
green bacon, uncooked about 10cm (4 inches) square
2–4 heads of garlic
2 large onions
2 large carrots
handful of flour
1 wineglass olive oil
3–4 cloves
Pinch of nutmeg
2 teaspoons sugar
1 tumbler *Prosek* (a Korculan sweet wine) or madeira or sweet sherry
1 cupful of soaked, stoned prunes (about a dozen)
3 tumblers of good home-made tomato *sugo*

Sugo
Fresh and/or tinned tomatoes, onions, celery, carrot, sugar, herbs, olive oil and good strong broth, all simmered together for several hours.

Marinade the beef in a bowl for 24 hours using enough wine vinegar to cover it. Turn the meat over once or twice during this period. Remove it and pat dry with a clean cloth. Cut up the garlic into thin slivers the length of the clove. Cut up the bacon into larding strips about 5cm (2 inches) long and the thickness of a pencil.

Make a deep slit in the side of the meat with a suitably narrow, sharp and pointed knife. Insert a piece of bacon and a sliver of garlic into this slit, pushing them both well into the centre of the meat. Continue larding all the way round the sides, and then see if you can fit in another row, maybe above or below the first one, but do not pierce the top or bottom surface of the meat.

When all the bacon and garlic is used up and the meat is fit to burst, put a large handful of flour on a plate and flour both sides of the fillet well. Chop the onions and carrots roughly and put them into a heavy iron and enamel casserole pan with a wineglassful of good olive oil. Add 3 cloves, a good pinch of nutmeg and 2 teaspoons of sugar. When the onions have softened, but not darkened, add the meat and sauté it well, turning it over several times until it is well coloured on every side. This will take at least 10 minutes. Add the tumbler of madeira-type wine and let it cook a little longer, turning it over once more.

Pour in at least 3 tumblers of good tomato *sugo*: enough to cover the meat well. Cook for a few minutes, then add the prunes, stir, and cover the pan. Continue until the meat is tender (roughly 2 hours); you can top up the sauce with more *sugo* or a little broth if necessary.

Take the fillet out and put it on a flat hot serving dish; slice it vertically about the thickness of a little finger, so each piece shows circles of larding.

Surround it with previously cooked potato gnocchi (or noodles), then pour half the sauce over the meat.

Pour the other half into a sauceboat (scraping the pan for all juices) and hand separately with a dish of grated Parmesan cheese for the gnocchi or pasta.

Potato gnocchi (serves 6–8)

120g (4oz) butter
300ml (½pt) milk
120g (4oz) flour
4 eggs
3–4 medium potatoes
30g (1oz) grated Parmesan or Gruyère cheese
salt and pepper

Melt the butter into the milk in a good heavy pan. Bring to boil and while boiling add the flour and keep stirring for 4–5 minutes. Take off stove and beat in the eggs one by one, then add the potatoes (which have been boiled and sieved), finally add the grated Parmesan or Gruyère, salt and pepper. Make small quantities of gnocchi from this paste using either two teaspoons or a forcing bag with 2.5cm (1 inch) nozzle. Poach them a few at a time in a large pan of fast-boiling salted water. When cooked they rise to the top. Drain and serve with melted butter and a little grated Parmesan. (This also makes a delicious first course with a creamy Mornay sauce on its own.)

Baked fruit

My husband loves compôtes and we now bake apples, pears and prunes the old-fashioned way, overnight at the bottom of a slow-cooking Aga. If you don't have a slow oven like an Aga or a Rayburn, one of those electric 'slow-cooking' casseroles would produce the same result. We eat it with a bowl of clotted cream, or a dish of *coeurs à la crème* or *Kefir* – a yogurt-like culture that we once brought back from the Caucasus and that has lived with us ever since. We feed it daily with cream, turning it into the best soured cream this side of Vienna.

Apples and pears
Have a low earthenware pot with a lid. Pare your fruit carefully, halve it and put in the pot. Strew over sugar (or honey) to taste. Add flavouring to taste (lemon juice and rind) then pour over 1 tablespoon water. Cover with the apple or pear peelings pressed carefully down on top of the fruit. Put on the lid and place in oven.

Prunes
Wash them first with boiling water before putting in the pot. Flavour with one or two cloves and 1.2–2.5cm (½–1 inch) stick of cinnamon. Add sugar to taste and about ½ a cupful of weak tea (or water), according to amount of fruit. Peel ½ a lemon and put the parings over the prunes in the same way as for apples and pears.

Compôte of apricots
The wild 'Persian' ones are the best, and good health shops or Asian delicatessens sell them. Wash and soak the dried fruit for 8 hours, then bake overnight with a little honey and lemon peel, as above, or stew them gently and briefly. Eat them with a dish of chilled soured cream.

Jane Martin

A Somerset Weekend

I am never bored with my kitchen – I don't see enough of it for that – so we meet for sessions like old friends, usually taking a weekend to catch up with each other. I do the same with my husband, children and friends as the life of a freelance film and television designer means long periods away from them and home.

The Somerset Levels, where we live, are not renowned for their culinary excellence. The only few square miles unconquered by the Danes in the ninth century are better known as the spot where Alfred burnt the cakes. What were once islands are now largely drained marshland, willow beds and apple orchards, and our house stands high on the bank of a tidal river, with a garden like a narrow stretch of ribbon that has been quite taken over by what has become known as the allotment.

My husband has a passion for growing enormous quantities of produce quite disproportionate to the size of our land and family, but as I have little time for, and detest, shopping, I am usually more than happy to pick or be picked for. I say usually. Sometimes my husband's tastes are rather too esoteric. Before now I've rummaged through the freezer, and turned what I've taken to be spinach into *oeufs florentine*, only to find that he's been on a secret gathering mission and frozen batches of nettles. All right in soup, but disgusting in *oeufs florentine*. He also freezes puffballs, which are very much an acquired taste! He's tried to introduce us to two things indigenous to Somerset, both of which failed. The first, snails, were found in the allotment and put in a bucket of sawdust for a few days. What looked like a witches' brew produced some shrivelled specimens that nobody could face eating, so now

118 JANE MARTIN

they're left to eat the lettuces. The other delicacy, eels, is never on the menu because he can never manage to catch them, although my stepson usually catches scores of six-inch ones when he comes to stay.

In the autumn we freeze 100kg (200lb) of tomatoes, and the rest hang ripening, Babylon-fashion, from hooks in the kitchen, barn and garden room, lasting through to Christmas, with the stubborn ones going into chutney. I pick them from above the kitchen table, and our weekenders get treated to gazpacho, salads and Bloody Marys made according to our own special recipe with fresh tomato juice.

Even in the kitchen every space is cultivated, and at any time of the year there is always something propagating, growing, climbing or ripening. Cucumbers trail up the window, and I work in a tropical jungle of pineapples, lemon trees smuggled from hotter climes, orange trees and date palms. We look out onto the river bank and our giant pumpkins. Once some river-walkers pinched one and the news got back to us that they'd thought it was a melon – divine justice when they dished it up!

Saturday is a good day for gathering together children, guests and dog, and a multitude of bags and baskets, and motoring off in our small dinghy, downriver to pick apples, upstream for wild mushrooms, blackberries, sloes and damsons. We return laden down with the ingredients for my rustic apple pie, which I serve with gooseberry ice cream, and a delicious raw blackcurrant and blackberry fool which always gets eaten with home-made wholemeal shortbread.

Choosing the wine is not difficult. My husband, besides being a somewhat unorthodox horticulturist, is a passionate viniculturist! The south side of our house is completely obscured by vines – Müller Thurgau and Seyve Villard. The harvest for the past three years has surpassed all expectations. From 12 bottles in 1979, we went to 48 the following year, and 1981, which is not yet bottled, should give us 120. Soon it will be a full-blown industry, not just a curiosity. We've finally invested in a wine press, which means my liquidiser might just manage to grind on for a bit longer. It survived the first two pressings, but now looks glaucous rather than clear.

'Curload carbonnade' (a personal version of *carbonnade*) is a great standby for Friday or Saturday dinner, as it can be marinaded in advance and left to cook slowly for as long as 4 hours without coming to grief. Likewise the fool, which I usually make from raw *frozen* blackcurrants, which are easy to purée without cooking, and fresh blackberries. I often make a delicious spinach and sesame salad, with garlic croûtons for Saturday lunch, a great post-Bloody Mary favourite with guests.

Our Sunday joint will be followed by the rather special 'rustic' apple pie already mentioned, christened by my two daughters, and the ice cream which I'm always forgetting to take out of the freezer in time, and which consequently needs a pickaxe to cut it. This, in particular, is the perfect accompaniment to Château Reid '79, of which we've still got a couple of bottles for special occasions.

What for most people is probably a typical weekend's cooking is a particular pleasure for me as I am away from home for so much of the year. After surviving hotel life and strange locations, it is the perfect contrast – as my husband's growing and bottling are for him – and for me it is the greatest possible relaxation.

Tomato juice (makes 4 pints)

2½kg (5lb) raw tomatoes
5 tablespoons sugar
1 teaspoon salt
2 tablespoons home-pickled nasturtium seeds
½ teacupful of pickling vinegar
2 cloves of garlic
generous dash of barbecue sauce or Tabasco

Liquidise and add vodka to taste.

Curload carbonnade (serves 6)

1kg (2lb) lean braising steak
90g (3oz) wholemeal flour
2 large onions
1 tin of tomatoes
250g (8oz) button mushrooms
2 cloves of garlic
2 small bottles Guinness
pinch of nutmeg
1 tablespoon muscovado sugar
salt and pepper

Chop meat into cubes and dust in seasoned wholemeal flour – cook gently in a very little dripping in casserole on top of cooker until brown. Add onions and cook for a little longer. Add remainder of flour, crushed garlic and seasoning. Stir around for about 2 minutes – add Guinness and equal amount of water, tin of tomatoes, nutmeg and sugar – bring to boil to thicken and then switch off and leave to marinate overnight.

Day of serving – bring back to boil on top of stove – add mushrooms which have been lightly tossed in a little melted butter.

Put in very slow oven (100°C/200°F, gas mark low) for anything up to 4 hours.

Spinach and sesame salad with croûtons
(serves 6)

500g (1lb) young leaf spinach
2 avocado pears
2 chopped hard-boiled eggs
60g (2oz) garlic croûtons
1 dessertspoon ground roasted sesame seeds
2 tablespoons olive oil
juice of 1 lemon
freshly ground black pepper

Make croûtons with wholemeal bread, using at least 3 cloves of garlic, fry in olive oil. Roast sesame seeds in medium oven for about 10 minutes or until nicely browned. Combine chopped avocado, hard-boiled eggs, sesame seeds, oil, lemon juice and seasoning.

Line a salad bowl with washed spinach leaves – heap avocado mixture on and sprinkle with croûtons and serve.

Gooseberry ice cream (serves 8)

1kg (2lb) green gooseberries (fresh or frozen)
2 tablespoons water
250g (8oz) castor sugar
300ml ($\frac{1}{2}$pt) double cream

Wash gooseberries (if fresh) place in saucepan (not necessary to top and tail them). Add water and sugar, simmer gently until fruit is soft – about 15 minutes.

Pour off some of the juice into separate jug – it can be added to purée later. Rub remaining fruit and juice through sieve to make thick purée. Allow to cool. Lightly whip the cream and fold into the purée. I add a few drops of green colouring to give a cool fresh colour.

Freeze for about 2 hours – until partially frozen – remove and whisk or beat until creamy and return to freezer in freezer container.

Wholemeal shortbread

120g (4oz) 100% wholemeal flour
60g (2oz) rice flour
60g (2oz) castor sugar
120g (4oz) butter

Blend all the ingredients – press mixture into ball and shape into a round cake about 1.2cm ($\frac{1}{2}$ inch) thick – crimp the edges, prick design on top – mark into sections using knife.

Bake in a slow oven (150°C/300°F, gas mark 2) until firm and golden brown – about 1 hour.

Dust with castor sugar while still warm, allow to cool before removing from baking tray.

Blackcurrant and blackberry fool
(9–10 ramekins)

500g (1lb) blackcurrants (frozen without sugar; thawed if frozen)
500g (1lb) blackberries
280g (10 oz) sugar
300ml ($\frac{1}{2}$pt) double cream

Place blackcurrants, blackberries and sugar in liquidiser and reduce to liquid, strain through nylon sieve. Whip cream – fold into blackberry and blackcurrant mixture. Dish into individual ramekins – either freeze or cool in fridge if serving same day.

When frozen allow to thaw at room temperature for 1 hour before serving.

Rustic apple pie (serves 8–10)

To fit 30cm (12-inch) diameter flan dish

370g (12oz) shortcrust pastry made with 100% wholemeal flour
1$\frac{1}{2}$kg (3lb) cooking apples
grated rind and juice of 1 lemon
60g (2oz) chopped almonds
60g (2oz) chopped walnuts
60g (2oz) mixed peel
60g (2oz) sultanas
60g (2oz) raisins
cinnamon and mixed spice to taste
180g (6oz) muscovado sugar

Line flan dish with $\frac{2}{3}$ of pastry. Peel and chop apples – put in flan dish and then add all other ingredients – roll out remaining $\frac{1}{3}$ of pastry and cover pie. Prick holes and decorate.

Cook in hot oven 220°C/425°F, gas mark 7 for 40 minutes. Allow to cool and freeze. Or allow to cool slightly and dust with castor sugar and serve.

To serve from frozen – allow to thaw and warm through in oven 120°C/250°F, gas mark $\frac{1}{2}$ for about 25 minutes and dust with sugar before serving.

The Countess Peel

A Riverside Barbecue

I've never been very good at eating formally. At dinner-parties, if I am enjoying the conversation, I get confused and then bored by the passing of many plates laden with sauce-disguised substances. At restaurants I always want to sample what other people have ordered because it invariably looks better than mine. I don't like cooking grand food either; it takes much longer to prepare than it does to eat. If it's fattening, people bear a grudge against you; if it is not, you can be quite certain that the ingredients cost the earth.

Perfectly suited to my taste is the Eastern method of presenting food. Flashing my chopsticks, I can sample and savour to my heart's delight without offending anyone, but still, top of my list comes the barbecue.

I don't mean that gleaming gun-metal, barrel-shaped structure built into the patio wall by the swimming-pool. I mean a good old driftwood bonfire that has burnt for many hours and has been allowed to subside into a beautifully scented pile of glowing embers. All I need is a couple of cake racks or a sheet of wire netting and I am ready to go. To me the essence of a barbecue is the flavour that a wood fire gives to meat, and anything else you choose to take along should merely be an accompaniment. One must not confuse it with a picnic. Gulls' eggs, smoked salmon, taramasalata, parma ham and melon are lovely, but keep them for another occasion. For the same reason, I am not a great advocate of strong sauces that detract from the very thing you have been striving to achieve. I love devilled and barbecue sauces, but prefer to keep them for the dull days when I have to grill things in my kitchen.

Gunnerside, set in one of the most beautiful National Parks in the country, would appear to offer ample opportunities for organising picnics out on the moors when we are shooting grouse, up in the old lead-mines, or down by one of the many waterfalls that guide the Swale towards the sea. But the weather is so seldom suitable that I never dare plan anything in advance, preferring to say simply 'we're on' when the time is right. We have had some glorious impromptu midsummer nights, turning the steaks until dawn. An hour away at Arkholme in Lancashire we have a second string to our bow, one that is less likely to be in the grip of monsoon-style rains like Swaledale.

Fishing is a notorious hunger- and thirst-inducing pastime. Actually, if everyone is hauling-in fish, grumbling stomachs are ignored, but if there hasn't been a single rise all morning, rumbles of bored petulant digestions become so audible that no flabby spam sandwich and thermos of tea are likely to fill spirit or stomach with cheer.

I can divide these fishing trips into two categories:

1. We are woken up at dawn by a telephone call from the gillie to the effect that the fish are taking. Hurtling out of bed grabbing everyone and anyone willing to go, I have five minutes to jam something edible into the car, while my husband cancels his business appointments on the pretext that something more important has cropped up.
2. Relations or friends decide to come and stay to fish. A definite date, no matter what the conditions, and I have time to prepare.

Plan one: my husband heads for the boot room and I make a dash for the kitchen. I keep my fingers crossed that he remembers my bag of 'foul weather gear'. If I don't use all the clothes, we can sit on them. If we don't need them, you can be quite certain we will require the insect repellent that has got to be at the bottom of one of those pockets, under the wrist warmers, fingerless gloves and woolly hats.

I attend to the first priority – the drink. Into a cold bag go two freezer packs, some Carlsberg Special Brew or cider, lots of red and white wine, and perhaps some home-made sloe or damson gin. If there are children coming, I add a bottle of Ribena and one of orange. I throw in the openers and things to drink out of, plus a jar of sugar and cream, and zip it up. Three thermoses are then filled with strong black coffee, milk and iced water.

Next, out with the hamper – or preferably a laundry basket. Plates, knives, forks, teaspoons, loads of paper towel, a sharp knife (that will immediately be commandeered to gut fish or cut birds' nests out of tangled casts), a fish slice, some kitchen tongs, a big salt and peppermill that won't get lost in the long grass, lots of pedal-bin liners for rubbish, and some long-handled forks for children to 'help'. Next the ketchup, mustard, chutney and home-made french dressing and 'cheat 1000-island' that live in jam jars in the fridge.

Then the food: $\frac{1}{2}$lb butter in a $\frac{1}{2}$lb butter-sized box, a big lump of cheese that won't run amok, a fruitcake in a tin, some apples in a bag, bars of chocolate (for fishermen's pockets) in another bag and packets of crisps. I have a large round tupperware salad-bowl with a lid. Into this I throw any fresh vegetables I can lay my hands on. There will be plenty of time to make a salad when we get there. A hard lettuce, avocados, fennel, cucumber, tomatoes, cauliflower, courgettes, watercress, chicory – anything that isn't mushy is suitable. Then I am ready to pull my standbys out of the deep-freeze. Bearing in mind that we have probably got about four hours until lunch or, in the case of seatrout, supper, for things to defrost, obviously a 4lb chicken would not be suitable. I select a bag of small wholemeal rolls that will crisp up nicely on the perimeter of the fire, a potato quiche, which is a special favourite of ours as it

A salmon barbecue

is equally good hot or cold and even better tepid, then boxes of hamburgers labelled 'children's' and 'grown-ups', a couple of packets of good not too fatty pork sausages, and I'm ready to go.

For *Plan Two* you have more scope but that just means more choice; you still want to keep it as simple as possible. Stick to the same accompaniments, making perhaps a more interesting salad, such as a *niçoise* and, to ring the changes, you might replace the rolls with garlic bread, and the quiche with baked potatoes, but you can never be sure how they are getting on once they are in the fire. The children will eat them no matter how charred the outside and raw the centre, but their indigestion on the journey back home might make you regret it.

Chicken comes into its own when cooked on an open fire. Best of all, if you can lay your hands on them, are the free-range. I roast mine at home for an hour, and then joint them and wrap them up, just finishing them off on the fire, as bloody bones are very off-putting, and it is a shame to blacken the delicious skin. Small birds such as partridge, grouse, poussins, quail and golden plover are ideal. Split them down the backbone and grill them flat, basting them frequently with butter or a favourite sauce.

Kebabs of lamb, skewered with quartered onions and tomatoes, whole button mushrooms, slices of green pepper and bay leaves are good, or turkey breasts with bacon rolls.

Fish that has just been caught tastes wonderful however you cook it, especially if you are the one who caught it! But if I am taking fish with me, I like to fillet it because bones getting chummy with the salad or flicked all over the rugs are a bore. Wrap up individual portions in buttered foil after stuffing them with a lump of butter, a slice of lemon, salt and pepper and any fresh herbs you have lying around. They only take about 20 minutes to cook.

Steak, I suppose, is the favourite and is best when marinaded for 24 hours. I trim off all the fat, put the steak in a freezer box and pour over the marinade, put on the lid, give it a shake every now and then, and only take it out when I am ready to put it onto the grill.

With experience I have learned that it is worth sticking to the old favourites. It's really not the time or place to experiment on your friends. The same applies to feeding children. If, like mine, they don't like anything that resembles 'skin', you can't blame them for being put off by half an inch of cinders. Why spoil their fun by forcing the more sophisticated game birds on them when all they really want are huge quantities of sausages and hamburgers?

Hamburgers (serves 4–6)

1kg (2lb) lean rumpsteak or chuck steak
1 small onion
a few sprigs of parsley
2 teaspoons Worcestershire sauce
salt and pepper
2 eggs
seasoned flour

Additions for adults
1 crushed clove of garlic
dash of Tabasco
a few capers, finely chopped
1 tablespoon brandy

Finely chop the meat, onion and parsley in a food processor. Add the remaining ingredients and blend for a moment. Remove the quantity required for children's hamburgers. Add the adults' additions to their hamburgers. Make handfuls of the mixture into balls. Roll in seasoned flour and flatten to about 1.2cm ($\frac{1}{2}$ inch) on a tray. Freeze and then pack in freezer boxes, layered between sheets of paper.

Potato quiche

4 large cold baked potatoes
2 tablespoons flour
60g (2oz) butter
salt and pepper
1 clove of garlic, crushed
nutmeg
120g (4oz) double cream (or single cream mixed with two egg yolks)
grated Gruyère cheese
120g (4oz) bacon
seasoned flour

Mash, mouli or sieve the potatoes and add the butter, flour and seasoning. Roll around in seasoned flour, put into a quiche dish and flatten out. Prick with a fork. Snip up the bacon and sprinkle on top, dab around the garlic, cover with cream, grate on a little nutmeg. Finish with a layer of cheese and bake until brown (200°C/400°F, gas mark 6) for about 20 minutes. When cold, wrap in foil and freeze.

Marinade for steak or lamb chops

enough red or white wine to cover the meat
2 tablespoons wine vinegar
1 small onion
1 carrot
some parsley stalks
1 bayleaf
a few peppercorns
sea salt
1 doz bruised juniper berries

Put the ingredients into a saucepan and bring to the boil. Allow to simmer for 10 minutes. Cool and add 2 tablespoons olive oil. Pour over the meat and leave for a few hours, or preferably overnight.

The Duchess of Roxburghe

A Scottish Grouse Shoot

At the turn of the century sport was the ruling country house passion, and Floors was no exception. To make absolutely sure that this enthusiasm was pursued to its utmost limits, it was necessary to spend as much time as daylight would permit out of doors, more often than not getting wet and extremely cold. My husband's American grandmother, appalled at the discomfort cheerfully borne by rather hardier British constitutions, created a picnic tradition envied by other Edwardian houses, which we try our hardest to maintain.

The American Duchess introduced individual silver boxes which we still use, heavily crested and with holders for knife and fork, and it was my mother-in-law who perfected the picnic lunch for a grouse shoot, substantial and delicious, with our first-class chef, Iain Collingbourne, as its creator.

At our grousemoor, Byrecleugh, in the lovely Lammermuirs, we settle down by the river Dye, and unwrap a typical lunch of egg or salmon croquettes, the latter totally fresh and liquid with cream, and crisp on the outside, or a delicious game pâté topped with wafer-thin bacon. We then turn to the silver boxes which contain two sorts of cold meat, cutlets covered in aspic, chicken, tongue, ham or beef, a fresh buttered bap or butter bun as they are called locally, a large slice of moist fruit cake, and biscuits for a lovely ripe and runny Brie or Stilton. Finally we include a veal and ham, or game pie, a large mixed salad and a few flaky pastry jam puffs or chocolate éclairs.

As the summer moves into autumn and the weather gets cooler, I sometimes find it more popular to have something hot, either a rich mixed game, or hare soup, or hot Cornish pasties in a flask. Later, during the pheasant shooting season, one of the day's shoots is a frozen, beautiful day's sport on the edge of the same moor. It looks (and feels) like Norway. The guns leave after breakfast with a flask of hot home-made

The Duchess of Roxburghe and Iain Collingbourne loading for lunch

sausages, and the girls join them at a keeper's house for lunch with a complete hot picnic, one of the favourite main courses being lamb crumble.

It may sound as if everything is smoothly organised and the picnics just materialise without fuss. It works on the whole, but there are very often last-minute panic-stricken dashes to Kelso, then the ever-anxious checking off of each item as it goes into the car. My husband is meticulous and likes everything perfect, and the miseries of leaving butter, pepper, mustard or salad dressing behind get blown up to mammoth proportions. On one awful occasion, when newly engaged, I set off to Byrecleugh alone, thinking I knew the way, and got hopelessly lost. I eventually arrived after a despairing journey around the hills, which to me in those days all looked exactly the same, to find a row of very hungry and cross-looking men pacing up and down in front of the lunch hut. To add insult to injury I also had the drink hamper with me. I was never late again!

The other thing I frequently get wrong is numbers. It's very important to have the correct numbers because of the boxes, but all too often either I miscount or the odd local gun turns up with a girlfriend in tow. Then at the moment of dishing out there is an agonising pause when a place is left empty. I usually try to laugh lightly and go into a deeply boring account of my latest diet, toying merrily with a little Stilton and trying not to look when a replete guest tosses an unwanted cutlet to a soulful-eyed labrador.

On the whole, however, the picnics are a lot of fun. They invariably involve far more work than a large dinner-party, but the atmosphere of a group of friends, children and dogs on a glorious day, is a party in itself, and one which we will always hope to continue.

Game pâté (serves 12)

4 game birds (pheasant or grouse)
310g (10 oz) ham
2 onions (sautéed)
90g (3oz) mushrooms (sautéed)
300ml ($\frac{1}{2}$pt) double cream
1 glass dry sherry
seasoning
6 rashers streaky bacon

Place the birds in a covered roasting dish with a liberal amount of butter and the ham. Cook in a medium oven for 1 hour for grouse, 1 hour and 15 minutes for pheasant. Remove the meat from the birds, and mince, along with the ham, except for the breast of one bird.

Place the minced meat in a bowl, and stir in the onion and sherry. Add the cream until a moist mixture is obtained. Some of the residue from the roasting dish may be added if the mixture is too dry.

Spread half the mixture in a buttered ovenproof dish. Cover this with the carved breast and the mushrooms. Spread over the rest of the mixture. Lay the streaky bacon on top and four or five knobs of butter. Bake in a hot oven for 20 minutes and cool.

Egg croquettes (serves 6)

600ml (1pt) thick béchamel sauce
6 hard-boiled eggs
3 tablespoons double cream
salt and pepper
flour
1 egg (beaten)
breadcrumbs

Prepare sauce by making a roux with 60g (2oz) butter, 60g (2oz) flour, and adding pre-heated milk. Cook to a thick sauce and cool. Chop eggs fairly fine and add to the sauce. Season and add cream.

Chill until the mixture handles easily. Shape as for potato croquettes. Dip in flour, then egg, then breadcrumbs. Fry in hot oil.

Can be served hot or cold.

A Scottish Grouse Shoot

A packed lunch

Lamb crumble (serves 6)

500g (1lb) roast lamb
185g (6oz) onions (chopped and sautéed)
185g (6oz) white bread crumbs
60g (2oz) Cheddar cheese (grated)
mixed herbs
parsley

Use the pan juices from the lamb, combined with flour and stock, to make a thick brown sauce. Mix into the sauce 120g (4oz) of the onion. Cut the lamb into 1.2cm ($\frac{1}{2}$-inch) cubes and place in an ovenproof dish. Pour on enough sauce to just cover the meat.

Mix the breadcrumbs, remainder of onion, parsley, seasoning and sprinkle over the meat. Bake for 40 minutes in a moderate oven.

Philippa Scott

A Mediaeval Feast

I think every meal is a celebration, no matter the inspiration or intention, or whether the fare is simple or grand. It is a statement, a very personal offering and sharing, a form of theatre, of communication. Every meal is creative, and expresses an attitude of the person who plans, prepares, assembles and presents it. There is a consideration of balance, a wish to please, a generosity. A meal is also often allied to seduction, whether in business or more intimate terms. Many of us (and this can also come into seduction, be it pre-, post- or frustrated!) console ourselves with food when things seem bleak, sometimes with comfort dishes which transport us back to our childhood.

My early childhood in India, travels in the Middle East, my work and studies, which demand constant submersion in colours, textures, smells and patterns, all influence the direction of my tastes. My life revolves around antiques and artefacts, and in particular textiles and costumes, which I collect, restore, buy and sell. I love spicy colours, spicy tastes, contrasts of textures, the refinement of skills which can be

happily juxtaposed with boldness, naiveté (or apparent simplicity, which is true refinement). I love sweetmeats stuffed with nuts, drenched in honey and flower waters, coffee spiked with mastic or cardamom, the secret surprise of the various types of *kibbeh*, which are shells or burghul and ground meat containing yet another type of meatball within the shell. These last are, I imagine, a lesser form of the spectacular beast-within-a-beast feast dishes. Other favourites include pistachio nuts, which I find very beautiful, the delicate kernels of sharp green peeping from the papery skins of crinkly midnight purple and flaking pink. I consider they are best eaten by cramming greedy handfuls into one's mouth, but they also enhance many recipes. Surely mint tea, served in a simple waisted glass, with pine kernels floating in it, is as elegant as any wine. In Persia it is said that each pomegranate fruit contains one seed which will take you to paradise. The fruit's inner harvest, with the appearance of almandine garnets, breaks into impeccable sections. Its ruby juice is sweet, the bitter beautiful skins gives an orange-brown dye, and the culinary uses are many.

One of my best food and travel memories is a springtime spent in Corfu, staying with a friend (and wonderful cook) Annie, and our respective children. She has a house high above the sea in the north of the island. Across the bay, on a clear day, it is possible to see the guns on the Albanian coast, and in the valley below her olive groves is an old beautiful ruined Venetian villa. The wild spring flowers were riotous, the more delicate originals of so many garden familiars. There were also tiny exotic orchids, mating frogs and turtles getting on with life in noisy celebration. We looked for *horta*, wild asparagus, but ended up buying it in the market. It grows grasslike in the higher reaches, and for a few short blissful weeks it is tender and succulent. The flavour is delicate and delicious, cooked simply with butter and a squeeze of lemon juice. We ate so well that spring, the freshest catches from the fishing village, tiny artichokes eaten whole and cooked with heavy green olive oil, dill and lemon; with crusty sesame bread dunked and mopped in the juices. I recently found some imported Greek sheep yogurt in Harrods, and my daughter Chloe and I feasted for several days, pouring Greek honey over it for breakfast, and spooning it over grilled and charred aubergine slices in the evenings.

I used to try to travel away at Christmas-time, because it lent the rather surreal feeling of being slightly out of time with the rest of one's accustomed world. It always felt like stolen time. One such Christmas I took a home-made Christmas pudding (my mother's) to share with a Turkish friend in Istanbul. My friend is a distinguished scholar of Ottoman history, and bears a striking physical resemblance to Gandhi, a point of some amazement to whoever shares a meal with him and observes his total lack of ascetic restraint. He eats huge quantities of food very rapidly, and with complete abandon. His joy over the Christmas pudding was wonderful. We steamed it in the least hygienic circumstances available (his kitchen) and he produced a long-hoarded and excellent bottle of brandy, with which we liberally anointed both pudding and ourselves. There was some confusion over dates, but this was somehow appropriate, and we celebrated a day or so early. The celebration was maintained as long as the pudding lasted (the brandy ran out first). Pudding and brandy were consumed to the repeated benediction '*Blessed* be the hands that made such a pudding!'.

When I was an art student in the sixties, I was entranced by a book called *À Rebours* by J. K. Huysmans. In this book, the character, Des Esseintes, gives a banquet to mourn the passing of his virility. Dinner was served on a black tablecloth. There were baskets of violets and scabious on the table. Food was served by negresses wearing only slippers and stockings of silver stuff embroidered with tears. The plates were bordered with black, and the meal included turtle soup, black rye bread, black olives, caviare, mullet *botargo*, black puddings, game cooked in dark sauces, truffle jellies, chocolate creams, plum puddings, pears in grape-juice syrup, mulberries and black heart cherries. I was enormously impressed by Des Esseintes and his sensual style!

There is of course a great deal of humour associated with the table. Gold and silver galleons were fashioned to sail down long tables laden with fruit and sweetmeats. Platters of pretend fruit and nuts, often sitting amid exquisitely sculpted and painted creepy crawlies can be seen in most stately home and museum collections. There are plates made like leaves, flowers, crumpled paper; teapots made like cauliflowers and cabbages; cow creamers; rabbit tureens; all manner of surprises and playful jokes. This is also the case with food. I considered recreating Pegasus, as described in *The Satyricon* (first-century AD Rome). This was a roast hare with wings attached, stuffed and decorated. He was presented with pastry quails stuffed with nuts and raisins and quinces stuck with almond slivers to look like sea urchins. I considered various ways to make a unicorn. In the end I decided to offer the Cockatrice, a mediaeval dish. I learnt about the Cockatrice from my mother, who also happens to have a missionary-style cooking pot large enough to cook the beast, and which I am fortunately able to borrow.

Cockatrice (serves 20–25)

1 large capon 4½kg (9lb) or more, plucked and drawn, having the feet and head left on
1 large buck rabbit (as large as possible), skinned and drawn, hind legs complete

Filling
2½kg (5lb) minced veal
1kg (2lb) minced ham
2 large chickens, cooked, remove and chop up the meat
4 whole eggs, beaten
herbs to give good flavour (parsley, thyme, etc)
500g (1lb) onions, finely chopped
fresh ground black pepper
salt to taste
500g (1lb) fine breadcrumbs
(although not in the original recipe, I add grated lemon peel)

Mix all these ingredients in a bowl.

Velouté sauce to coat
120g (4oz) plain flour
120g (4oz) butter
900ml (1½pt) chicken stock made from the bones of the 2 chickens

If you want the beast more dragon-like, chopped *fines herbes* could be added to the velouté sauce to make it green.

Decoration
600ml (1pt) aspic, made up and cooled to setting point
sliced mushrooms, or carrots, whatever you want to make scales or feathers
gold paint for claws and head
scarlet paint or nail varnish for beak, cockscomb and claw ends
wooden skewer to attach head to body
gold-lace paper doileys, for ruff and wings
cocktail sticks

It is advisable to boil the capon's head and claws separately. (Or substitute a fine cockerel's head, or a goose head for dragon.) Cook them very gently.

Proceed to bone out the body by cutting the skin along the back and working beneath the flesh along the bone structure. Leave the legs complete with the lower bone.

Cut the rabbit behind the forelegs and bone out the body, retaining the bones in the hind legs. The lower leg joints will have fur on so wrap foil around these.

Lay both the carcases out flat on a table and with thin string sew them together. This string will be removed before decorating. Put the stuffing into the carcase and mould it. The beast should have 4 legs coming forward. Sew up the opening. Wrap the whole in a clean cloth and secure it well to keep its shape. Place it in a large pan, cover with cold water, add salt, peppercorns, bay leaves and any vegetables for flavouring the stock. Bring to the boil and simmer gently for about 3 hours. Allow to cool in the water. Next day take out and drain. When it is quite cold remove the cloth and refrigerate for 12 to 24 hours. The beast can either be lightly roasted and given a brown aspic glaze, or coated with a cream velouté sauce and decorated as suggested.

Serve on a bed of greenery, with gilded head and red cockscomb, red beak, gilded claws, golden ruff and wings secured with cocktail sticks.

A suitable accompaniment to the Cockatrice would be:

Bird's nest salad

cream cheese (Philadelphia, Boursin, whatever is available)
herbs
salt and black pepper
any desired food colouring
lettuce leaves, broken walnuts, flowers, for nest

Fashion egg shapes from cream cheese. Add herbs or colouring to some of the mixture for other types of eggs. Fleck with black pepper. Arrange on salad nest. Nasturtium or marigold petals would be a suitable addition to the basic salad.

A plate of quails' eggs could be served with them.

Aushak

This is an Afghan dish, like a ravioli with leek filling. It is served with two sauces, one (*chaka*) a yogurt sauce, the other one a meat and tomato sauce (*qeema*).

A simple flour and water pasta dough

Filling
chopped leeks
salt
some cayenne pepper

Sauce Chaka
Drained yogurt mixed with fresh ground garlic and salt.

Sauce Qeema
Minced beef, lamb, or a mixture of both, cooked with chopped onion and tomato (tinned will do) – brown and reduce to a thick sauce.

Roll out dough, and either use a ravioli mould, or cut out shapes with pastry cutters. A popular Afghan shape is a circle, which is filled, one side turned over the filling and sealed and crimped, and the whole thing is then curved round slightly, almost like tortellini. Drop these into boiling water or stock, and after 10 minutes remove, drain, and arrange on top of half the *chaka* in the serving dish. Cover with the remaining *chaka*, and top with chopped or dried mint. Put the meat sauce over the whole thing and serve at once.

Orange flower cream (serves 6–8)

This was popular in the seventeenth and early eighteenth centuries.

Boil 3.6 litres (3 quarts) of water with castor sugar and the yellow rind, and juice of two lemons. Beat 8 eggs into 1.2 litres (2 pt) of cream, and pour it in. Stir very slowly in one direction only. Let it stand. Skim off the curd into a pierced dish to drain, and when it has set turn it out and pour round it lightly whipped cream which has been flavoured with orange flower water. Decorate with leaves of scented geranium, flowers, etc.

Gilt gingerbread (makes ordinary cake-size amount)

The original gingerbread seems to have been a type of solid honey cake, decorated and presented to look like leather armour, which was quilted and studded. It was a popular gift to exchange in the days of tournaments.

Cockatrice

1.750kg (3½lb) flour
750g (1½lb) honey
250g (½lb) butter
½ nutmeg grated fine
1 tablespoon ground ginger
1 tablespoon baking powder (unless self-raising flour is used)

Melt the honey with a little hot water, or in a bain-marie. Add melted butter, and mix with dry ingredients. Roll out, or press into a greased mould.

Bake for about 20 minutes in a warm oven.

To decorate. Paint unbeaten egg white and lay on edible gold leaf. It is harmless and a little goes a long way. Decorate with gilt-headed cloves driven in like studs, or *fleur de lys* (bay or box leaves).

Fresh melon and peach salad (serves 4)

This has an unusual and very refreshing taste. Do not let the salt put you off trying it.

1 melon
2 peaches
salt
sugar
lemon juice
5 tablespoons rosewater
crushed ice

Cut melon in half and make as many melon balls as possible. Put in a deep bowl, pour any residue of juice over them, and toss with salt. Peel the peaches and cut into half-inch slices. Add the peaches, sugar, lemon juice and rosewater to the melon, and toss them about gently to mix well. Cover tightly and refrigerate for at least 2 hours. Serve in individual dishes with crushed ice.

Do not overdo the salt; a little goes a long way.

Fortune Stanley

Cooking in Cumbria

My introduction to cooking began very early at about the age of nine. My mother had always been determined that my sister and I should become efficient cooks, so, as one way of achieving this, a Baby Belling was put on the end of the oak table in the dining-room. She and anyone kind enough to cook for us would instruct us in the method of making a macaroni cheese and apple charlotte – I wonder why these especially. A wonderful Scottish cook joined our family when I was four, and ten years later, during the war, we had proper, serious lessons with her in the kitchen.

Eventually I married and acquired a large kitchen at Witherslack in Cumbria. We now have a large collection of cookery books, and my husband is very appreciative of interesting recipes. He has somewhat complicated my life by insisting on a first course for luncheon and dinner – for choice, not soup. He defends his request by saying that he is a disciple of the 1st Viscount Norwich, who maintained that there are only a limited number of luncheons in one's life and a bad one is an opportunity missed.

Our house is just inside the Lake District National Park, though some way from the lakes themselves. Among local supplies are fresh shrimps and fish from Morecambe Bay, together with damsons that grow more or less wild and can be bottled or deep-frozen. The garden keeps us in vegetables and herbs for most of the year, my husband's farm producing pork, eggs, butter and splendid cream. We keep to a fairly standard pattern of entertaining, with a substantial first course in place of hors d'oeuvres or soup. At luncheon the main course will usually be followed by a pudding if children are in the party, or cheese (such as Blue Wensleydale), or nothing but coffee. We never exceed three courses at dinner. Occasionally I make a point of serving a dish particularly to somebody's liking: oatmeal pancakes to a daughter-in-law with a particular taste for them, or sweetbreads to a neighbour who never tires of eating them however they are cooked.

Roulette of mushrooms (serves 4)

Suggestions are made for a sauce which should be prepared beforehand; but avoid strong flavours like tomato.

350g (12oz) mushrooms
30g (1oz) butter
1 rasher bacon, cut 4 or 5 times
1 onion 115g (4oz)
15g (½oz) flour
½ clove garlic
20ml (1 tablespoon) double cream
3 eggs separated
425ml (¾pt) Madeira or Mornay sauce

Throw the bacon rasher, rind removed, into boiling water, boil for 2 minutes, drain, allow to cool and chop. Cook it in butter until crisp and then the finely chopped onion until translucent but not brown. Work in the flour and crushed garlic, cooking 2 minutes more. Add the finely chopped mushrooms and stir for about 3–4 minutes; when slightly reduced pour in the cream and continue cooking to form a purée. Transfer to a large mixing bowl, allow to cool, and stir in 2 of the 3 egg yolks, discarding the third. Season.

Have ready a pre-heated moderate oven (180°C/350°F, gas mark 4). Line a swiss-roll tin, about 30 × 22cm (12 × 9 inches) with buttered greaseproof paper, or better, a non-stick paper such as Bakewell. Whip the egg whites until stiff, with a pinch of salt and fold them into the mushroom mixture with a perforated spoon. Quickly pour the mixture over the paper and spread it as evenly as possible. Bake at once in the oven for *10 minutes only*.

Lay a cloth, such as a linen napkin or a clean drying cloth, over the soufflé; then, stretching it tight at the ends, turn the tin over, remove the tin and strip off the paper. With hands under the cloth, roll up but not too tightly. Transfer this roulette to a hot serving dish, not lifting but rolling, and pour along the spine a Madeira or Mornay sauce, already made hot. Serve as soon as possible, cutting across into slices. Serve about half the sauce in a warm boat; the object of pouring some of it over is to keep the roulette hot, since being a kind of soufflé it is liable to collapse when cold.

Pickled pork (serves 6–8)

This quantity of pickle should serve for a boned loin of 5lb (2.3kg) cut across into two equal pieces, one of which is eaten hot. The other, after cooking, is a *jambon blanc*, unsmoked ham, which keeps for more than a week if wrapped in foil and stored in a refrigerator. The 'cure' is based on Bradenham and Suffolk hams, with more sugar than salt, and plenty of juniper.
(Pickling time 5–7 days)

Note: A glass or glazed earthenware dish is needed for this recipe.

1.2kg (2½lb) boned and rolled loin of pork
180g (6oz) light brown sugar
120g (4oz) sea or rock salt (*not* table salt)
15–20 juniper berries
5–6 allspice (whole)
5–6 peppercorns
1 bay leaf
2 sprigs of thyme (or 1 teaspoonful dried mixed herbs)
1 level teaspoonful saltpetre (potassium nitrate)
olive oil

Start preparing this pickle the day before it is wanted. Dissolve the sugar and salt in about 2.3 litres (4pts) of hot water. Stir in the roughly crushed juniper berries, allspice and peppercorns, with the bay leaf and thyme. Bring back to the boil, simmer 4–5 minutes, allow to cool (covered with a cloth) and stand overnight. The pickle must be quite cold.

Next day score the pork fat for eventual roasting (unless the butcher has done it). Lay the meat in a glass or glazed earthenware dish or crock, into which it will fit fairly snugly. Sprinkle with the saltpetre (which corrodes metal). Strain the pickle over the meat and allow to stand, covered, in a cool place for five to seven days (loin) or eight to ten days (boned shoulder or leg). Stir and turn every day. The joint may need weighting down with a glazed plate. If there is not enough liquid to just cover the meat, add more water with a tablespoonful or two of salt and sugar.

When needed, rinse the meat in cold water and put it into a saucepan with enough water to cover, and a small sliced onion and carrot (optional) – but no salt.

Bring just to the boil and *simmer* for 30 minutes (loin) or 50 minutes (leg or shoulder). Drain and dry the meat, discarding the vegetables. Rub the meat all over with olive oil and lay it in an oiled roasting tin, rind side upwards. Rub the rind with salt and bake in a hot oven 220°C/425°F, gas mark 7 for 35–45 minutes, basting at half time. Eat hot or cold.

Oatmeal pancakes (serves 6)

120g (4oz) fine oatmeal
30g (1oz) butter
2 eggs
150ml (¼pt) milk
300ml (½pt) soda water from bottle or siphon

Just melt the butter over a very low heat, and keep warm. Put the oatmeal into a bowl, making a well in the centre. Break the eggs into the well, drop in a pinch of salt, add a little milk and stir. Continue stirring and adding milk until all is used up. Then stir in the melted butter and beat or whisk until smooth. Set aside for 20 minutes, so that the oatmeal can absorb water; leave for longer if convenient. Immediately before use stir in the soda water, but do not beat or whisk.

These pancakes, which are very thin and 'see-through' are most easily made in a very hot non-stick pan, about 15–18cm (6–7 inches) diameter at the base. It is useful to have a ladle containing about 2 tablespoons, from which the right quantity, about 1½ tablespoons, can readily be judged. Oil the pan at the beginning and at intervals with the merest trace of butter, rubbed on with a small piece of greaseproof paper. After pouring in the batter, and distributing it evenly, cook on one side for about 1 minute; then toss, or turn over with a spatula, and finish for about ½ minute. Drain on kitchen paper. Enough for about 15 pancakes (the first couple or so in a batch may well turn out badly, even in trained hands).

With pieces of greaseproof paper between, and packed in a polythene bag, these pancakes can be deep-frozen, and keep well for a month or so. To thaw, put them between two plates and heat gently, over a pan of simmering water or in a very low oven.

Of course, the same amount of plain flour as oatmeal can be used. If served sweet, scatter with sugar and lemon juice, as usual.

Shrimps in oatmeal pancakes (serves 6)

500g (1lb) fresh or potted shrimps
80–100ml (4–5 tablespoons) béchamel sauce
12 oatmeal pancakes
melted butter
30g (1oz) grated cheese

The pancakes will have been prepared first.

Next make about 150ml (¼pt) béchamel sauce, rather more than will be needed; it can be flavoured with a few drops of anchovy essence or the grated rind of half a lemon, its purpose being chiefly to bind the shrimps together.

Over a very low heat mix the shrimps (washed free from sand in a colander, drained, and patted dry with a clean cloth) with just enough béchamel sauce to form a sticky mass; season with pepper. Continue heating gently, stirring with a fork, so that the whole is warmed through but not made hot – for fear of toughening the shrimps.

Have ready a hot serving dish, together with about 30–60g (1–2oz) of melted butter and the grated cheese. Distribute the warmed shrimps over the pancakes, roll up and arrange in the dish which has been brushed over with the butter. Along the spine of each pancake brush over a streak of butter, followed by a sprinkle of the grated cheese. Bake in a hot oven about 220°C/425°F, gas mark 7 for 10–15 minutes, until crisp and brown.

If potted shrimps are used, remove the butter on the top, or most of it. Frozen shrimps are tasteless and a waste of money.

Sauce soubise (serves 6)

1 large onion
30g (1oz) butter
15g (½oz) flour
300ml (½pt) milk
½ bay leaf
small pinch of sugar
20ml (1 tablespoon) single cream

Chop the onion roughly, not too fine; throw into boiling salted water, bring back to the boil and allow to blanch for 1 minute. Drain. Cook in the butter, with the bay leaf and small pinch of sugar, until translucent. Remove the bay leaf, work in the flour and cook gently for 2 minutes; pour in the cold milk and stir until smooth and boiling. Simmer for 10–15 minutes and then, off the heat, add the cream. When cold, whizz in a blender or processor, and season. Make hot when needed.

After the addition of cream, plunge the saucepan into a large bowl of cold water, and stir until the sauce is only just warm. Apart from anything else, such as preventing a skin on top, there is a considerable saving of time.

Sweetbreads soubise (serves 6)

Note: most cookery books give times of cooking for calves' sweetbreads, which are larger, more expensive but more delicious.

1kg (2lb) lambs' sweetbreads
1 small onion
1 small carrot
15g (½oz) butter
2 teaspoons flour
½ bayleaf
small sprig of thyme
parsley stalks
150ml (¼pt) dry white wine
300ml (½pt) soubise sauce

Soak the sweetbreads in several changes of lightly salted water to remove blood. Drain, cover with salted water and bring just to the boil; simmer 2–3 minutes, removing any scum, and drain again. Put into cold water. When cool, drain and remove gristle, connective tissue, etc.

Melt the butter in a saucepan large enough to contain the sweetbreads comfortably. Gently cook the sliced onion and sliced carrot, with the herbs, for 4–5 minutes; work in the flour and cook 2 minutes more. Lay the sweetbreads on this bed of vegetables, pour over the dry white wine and season lightly. Bring just to the boil and simmer, covered, for 30 minutes. Remove the sweetbreads to a warm serving dish, leaving the vegetables etc behind. Strain the liquid, add to the soubise sauce and make hot but do not boil. Adjust seasoning. Pour the sauce over the sweetbreads and serve.

Damson summer pudding (serves 8)

1.5kg (3lb) damsons
½ loaf white bread
250g (8oz) sugar

This pudding should be made the day before it is needed. If using fresh or deep-frozen damsons put a few teaspoonfuls of water into a saucepan – or if bottled the same amount of their juice – adding the damsons (without removing their stones) and allowing them to sweat, very slowly, over low heat. As the juice begins to be visible give an occasional stir. After about 1 hour the fruit should be becoming soft. Then add the sugar.

Meanwhile cut slices about 6mm (¼ inch) thick from a large white loaf, removing the crust. With them line the sides and bottom of a pudding basin or 15cm (6-inch) soufflé dish, capacity about 1.5 litres (2½pt). If possible the bottom of the dish should be covered with a circle of bread; fill any holes or joints with small pieces of bread to make a complete casing.

When the fruit is tender, take off the fire and, after cooling for 10 minutes or so, strain off the juice and reserve it. Pack the damsons into the prepared dish, covering the top with bread, and put on a saucer or plate weighted down quite heavily – 2.5kg (5lb) weight – overnight in a cool place or refrigerator. When needed, turn out on a serving dish, spooning over some of the reserved juice so that the pudding is a uniform purple all over, and surround with a little juice. Serve with single cream.

Christina Strutt

A Summer Picnic

Before I was married I lived in a tall red house in London with Christopher Sykes and his sister Henrietta. Christopher so impressed me with his cooking, giving grand and glorious dinner-parties, that I quietly survived on bacon sandwiches, thus avoiding any sort of competition with my landlord.

As a novice country wife, I spent my time reading cookery books and preparing lavish feasts for my new husband. Six months and two stones later, I decided that a revolution must take place in the kitchen. Steamed puddings were replaced with brown rice and dull salads, crusty home-made loaves with dry crispbread. Two weeks later and not an ounce lighter, the time came for a second revolution. I decided that good fresh healthy food need not be as dull as brown rice and naked salads, but with little effort, a dash of imagination and a large garden, simple food can look and taste delicious.

Now the very best part of my little kitchen is when it expands and extends into the garden, when the summer months lure me to the vegetable patch rather than to the crowded shops of Bath.

I can think of no greater luxury than being able to live off the land. Fatness and impecuniosity were two very good reasons for leading us up the garden path to plough an acre of jungle, dig three ponds and 'take in' fourteen sheep, thus feeding ourselves and countless others on the fruits of these exercises. We have managed to rear freshwater crayfish in the ponds and on investigation have even found some quite respectable trout in the stream that runs at the bottom of the garden. I have often been tempted to rear our lambs on a diet of fresh mint, garlic and redcurrant jelly, to

save time when cooking them, but I was told that when cows were fed strawberries, their milk was not strawberry-flavoured, so it is doubtful whether my method would work.

But growing, catching and cultivating is only the beginning of the fun – which continues in the kitchen and ends deliciously on the lunch table – preferably outdoors and garnished with all the flowers you can muster. All the recipes given can be prepared in advance, which is a pretty good reason for trying them whether they make your mouth water or not!

Chilled lettuce soup (serves 4)

This soup should be served straight from the fridge and garnished with freshly chopped parsley and a touch of double cream.

2 or 3 lettuces
1.8 litres (2pt) chicken stock
60g (2oz) butter
small carton double cream
parsley
salt and fresh black pepper

Melt butter in a large saucepan. Wash and chop lettuce coarsely and throw into foaming butter. Cover with a tightly fitting lid and after about 5 minutes, when it has reduced substantially, add chicken stock and season to taste. Simmer for 10 minutes. Allow to cool. Put the soup into a liquidiser and whizz until smooth. Add cream reserving some for serving. Chill until needed.

Nothing could be simpler for a summer luncheon than a large selection of salads. Apart from the following recipes, I often serve the following favourites:

Peeled tomatoes with fresh basil and real mozzarella (not the vacuum-packed variety) dressed with vinaigrette.

Raw mushroom salad with olive oil, pepper, oregano, lemon juice and garlic.

Trout salad with almonds (serves 4)

4 medium-sized trout
1 glass white wine
90g (3oz) flaked almonds
2 oranges, peeled and chopped
1 avocado pear
2 bunches watercress
1 large celery heart
fresh tarragon
1 lemon

Wash and gut the trout. Lay in a baking dish lined with enough foil to enclose the trout. Pour over them the wine and sprinkle with tarragon, a few of the almonds, salt and pepper and lay a slice of lemon on each. Cover tightly with foil and poach in a hot oven for 15 minutes. When cool, very carefully bone the fish and break into pieces. Place the almonds on an ovenproof dish and grill for a few minutes until golden brown. Allow to cool. Wash and dry the celery and chop coarsely, chop the orange, avocado and tarragon.

Put all ingredients into a bowl and toss with either a dressing made of:
1 teaspoon Dijon mustard
6 tablespoons olive oil
2 tablespoons tarragon vinegar
1 teaspoon soft brown sugar
squeeze of lemon
salt and black pepper

Shaken in a jam jar – not stirred.

Or with a green mayonnaise made of:
2 egg yolks
1 teaspoon wine vinegar
150ml (¼pt) olive oil
salt and pepper
1 teaspoon lemon juice
1 tablespoon chopped parsley
1 tablespoon chopped chervil
1 tablespoon chopped tarragon

Put the egg yolks into a liquidiser, switch on to slow speed and add vinegar and lemon juice, and very, very slowly pour in the olive oil in a steady stream. Add salt and pepper to taste.

Put all the leaves of the fresh herbs into a colander and pour *boiling water* over them, then run them under the cold tap and pat dry in kitchen paper. Pound to a paste in a mortar and then put them through a sieve. Add this purée to the mayonnaise and mix well.

Freshwater crayfish (serves 4)

Catch some crayfish from your pond – or buy them from your fishmonger!

Wash them thoroughly in plenty of cold water and gut them by removing the intestinal tube very carefully so as not to break it; it is very important to remove all of it as any remains will cause the fish to have a bitter taste. Cook the crayfish in a *court-bouillon* consisting of a large onion and carrot finely chopped and gently cooked in 45g (1½oz) butter. Add 900ml (1½pt) of white wine and about 600ml (1pt) of water, a bouquet garni and bring to the boil. Simmer gently for 30 minutes. Throw in the cleaned crayfish and cook for 10 minutes.

Cool, and serve with either green mayonnaise or a garlic mayonnaise.

Champagne sorbet (serves 4)

If you are a greedy and impatient person this recipe can be followed up to the freezing instructions, when it can be served as a delicious (and very rich) summer drink, though your guests might be a little surprised at being served a drink rather than a pudding.

600ml (1pt) sugar syrup
1 glass dry white wine
2 glasses champagne
1 tablespoon brandy
juice of one lemon and one orange
double cream

Put all the ingredients into a large saucepan and bring to the boil for a few seconds. Cool to room temperature and add a large carton of double cream. Mix well and place in the freezing compartment of the refrigerator. When it has begun to freeze (about 3 hours) put the sorbet into the liquidiser and whizz for a few seconds until all the ice particles have disappeared. Return to freezer. Before using leave in the fridge to thaw slightly. Serve with strawberries or raspberries and:

Tuiles aux amandes

90g (3oz) butter
120g (4oz) castor sugar
45g (1½oz) plain flour
juice and grated rind of 1 orange
210g (7oz) flaked almonds

Cut up butter in a warm bowl. Mis in sugar until light and fluffy. Sift in flour and beat well. Add orange juice, rind and chopped almonds. Drop in teaspoonfuls onto a greased baking dish quite far apart as these tuiles spread. Bake at 200°C/400°F, gas mark 6 for 4–5 minutes. While still hot place on a rolling pin to curl and leave to cool. Finish cooling on a wire rack and store in an airtight container until needed.

Strawberries in fondant (serves 4)

This is a fairly complicated recipe but it is well worth the effort.

180g (6oz) castor sugar
200ml (⅓pt) water
good pinch of cream of tartar
vanilla essence
strawberries

Stir sugar, water and cream of tartar over a medium heat in a medium-sized saucepan. Stop stirring when the sugar mixture boils. Boil until mixture reaches soft ball stage or 118°C (240°F) on a sugar thermometer. Scrape out onto a wet marble slab and leave to cool. Knead mixture until a creamy consistency. Knead in essence and leave to rest in a bowl covered in a damp cloth for an hour. Place fondant mixture in a bain-marie and when fondant has completely melted, dip in strawberries using tongs, and place on a tray of sieved icing sugar to set.

Caroline Waldegrave

A Sophisticated London Dinner

It may seem odd in a professional cook who spends all day surrounded by food and cookery, but there is almost nothing I find more enjoyable than cooking a fairly sophisticated dinner-party for about sixteen people. In fact, I find it rather calming after a hectic day of sixty-four students all of whom have immensely different, but almost equally important crises, ranging from burnt caramel to horrid boyfriends, at exactly the same time.

As a working mother married to an MP, I have to be highly organised. Preparation can take several days and I enjoy it. I hate chaos and could never contemplate greeting my guests knowing that there was a mountain of washing-up in the kitchen and that I still hadn't put clean towels in the bathroom. Nor can I cope with that last-minute panic: 'Surely I gave them the same menu when they last came to dinner' and 'Oh my goodness, didn't the Smiths come with the Jones' just before Christmas'. To avoid this, I have a Smythson's menu book in which I keep careful lists of who came to dinner, on what dates, what they ate and who they sat next to. I also try to choose a

menu that can be prepared in advance, that is, the night before, and dishes that can either be served cold, are cooked at the last minute, or will sit contentedly while you wait wondering whether the last couple has broken down, got lost or just forgotten to come. Of course, even the best-laid plans go awry. Sometimes the plan itself is the cause of the trouble. So far (touch wood) I have had more trouble with guests than with food. One memorably uncomfortable evening derived from an attempt to bring together round one table all our small supply of media and literary friends. One or two were genuine stars; all considered themselves to be; none liked the presence of the others. Moral: one TV personality is enough; and if you know two writers, check that one has not just reviewed the other's latest novel, viciously, the week before.

My husband is a politician and so I feed plenty of MPs. Here the danger is the opposite: politicians behave like starlings – they flock together and all talk at once. More than a couple at a time can swamp any dinner. One at a time they are much nicer than you expect – though they also drink more than you expect. With bridge players (we play enthusiastic kitchen bridge) the skill is to balance playing standards as well as everything else – and somehow get your partner into a contract which makes you dummy just before you call people to eat. Journalists, of course, are the worst hazard of all: if disaster befalls, you run the risk of reading all about it in the public prints. Only the most honourable ring up and ask first. The nicest guests? The answer may be a surprise. Nothing is more fun than to have another cook to dinner. Jossy Dimbleby or Prue Leith will know everything you have been through, and sympathise. They know the agony of hearing the departing guest's opinion: 'Well *really, I could have done that myself.*'

I never plan precisely what we are going to have as one is inevitably dependent on what is in the shops. There are, however, a few basic rules that I keep in mind as I browse. I try to get a menu in which no ingredients are repeated and one which varies in colour, texture, seasonings and sauces. I try to avoid giving my guests too rich a meal; a rich main course, such as fillet of beef *en croûte* followed by *crème brûlée* would intimidate the most courageous of stomachs. You should feel full but not uncomfortable after a good meal. I try and avoid varying the style too much. The leap from a Provençal dish like *bouillabaisse* to, say, the English nursery (for example, bread and butter pudding) can be a bit alarming.

Two more recent innovations have made preparing and cooking dinner parties much easier. Firstly *nouvelle cuisine* (not that I am a devout devotee) dictates that it is pretty and charming to 'plate' food individually. It always used to be thought of as a caterer's short cut and not for home cooking. Practically, this means that you can plate up the first course and pudding well in advance and concentrate on the main course at the last minute. And when you have cooked the main course it too can be plated up in the kitchen, so that you don't need waitresses (just a noble husband) and the food stays hot. Secondly, the microwave oven. I know that microwaves can ruin delicious food but they are invaluable for reheating pre-cooked vegetables. I undercook (usually steam) a julienne of assorted vegetables such as carrots, turnips, leeks and courgettes, cool them under running cold water, drain them well and tip them into a huge serving dish. I then brush them well with melted butter, cover them with clingwrap and refrigerate them overnight. The next day the dish, clingwrap and all, is put into the microwave and heated up for five minutes.

On the day of the dinner-party, I rely on two people other than myself. My nanny copes with all the incidentals which can cause unbearable flaps – the clean towels, the coffee tray, the ice, the glasses, the flowers, the loo paper, the soap, etc, and my husband lays the table and organises the drink. At 6.00 pm I get home from work and only have to do the cooking. I plate up the first course and pudding, put the vegetables into the microwave, get out saucepans for the potatoes, gravy and sweet onion purée, get a couple of frying pans out for the collops, and set up the coffee in my wonderful machine (a Melitta 151), which means that all I have to do is turn on a switch as the pudding goes into the dining-room.

If my precision planning has worked, I can trot off and have a bath at about 7.15 and be changed and downstairs by 7.45 in time for a fairly relaxed drink before the doorbell goes. The only thing that can't be done in advance, however well organised you are, is the washing-up!

I should finally add that this type of food is the exception in the Waldegrave household. During the normal course of the week we are rational health-food lovers. That is to say, we indulge ourselves in the occasional dramatic binge but spend most of our time eating sensibly and avoiding large quantities of fat, sugar and salt.

Collops of lamb with sweet onion purée
(serves 4)

3 × 5 boned best ends of lamb, chined
fresh mint
30g (1oz) unsalted butter

For the purée
2 large spanish onions, finely chopped
85g (3oz) butter
1 teaspoon castor sugar

For the gravy
2 sticks celery
2 sprigs of fresh thyme
½ onion
2 teaspoons redcurrant jelly
1 tablespoon port
1 tablespoon orange juice
a little extra fresh thyme
1 generous teaspoon arrowroot

Set the oven to 200°C/400°F, gas mark 6.

With a small sharp knife remove the 'eye' of the best ends in one piece. Trim away any fat. Slice into 12 collops or steaks. Place in a bowl with plenty of chopped mint, cover and refrigerate overnight.

Cut away all the remaining meat and fat from the best ends, it can be used for barbecueing. Put the bones into a roasting pan and bake in the hot oven for ¾ hour or until well browned.

Meanwhile, prepare the onion purée. Melt the butter, add the finely chopped onions and cook very slowly until completely soft and brown but *not* burnt. This should take at least 45 minutes – it may even take an hour – add the sugar. Liquidise or whizz in a food processor until completely smooth. Season to taste with salt and white pepper.

When the lamb bones are well browned remove them, with as little fat as possible, into a large saucepan. Cover with 1.1 litres (2pt) water. Add the celery, onion and thyme. Bring slowly up to the boil skimming off the scum. Simmer for 1½ hours – skimming it every so often. Strain into a clean pan. It should measure 425ml (¾pt) – if it is more, reduce by boiling rapidly. Add the redcurrant jelly, port, orange juice and extra thyme leaves. Boil rapidly for 3 minutes. Mix the arrowroot with a little cold water, add some of the hot stock and return the mixture to the saucepan and bring up to the boil, stirring continually, and boil for no more than 1½ minutes. Taste and season with salt and pepper.

The next day reheat the sweet onion purée and

Fish terrine with chive and lemon dressing (top); collops of lamb with sweet onion purée (middle); fresh fruit salad with mango and passion fruit sauce (bottom)

gravy (without boiling). Fry the collops in hot unsalted butter for 2 minutes a side. Spoon a little gravy onto each diner's plate, put the collops on top of the gravy and place a spoonful of the purée on top of each.

Fish terrine with chive and lemon dressing
(serves 8)

This recipe is very quick to make in a food processor.

340g (12oz) filleted sole
340g (12oz) peeled prawns
2 teaspoons green peppercorns
1 large carrot peeled
45g (1½oz) french beans, topped and tailed
2 teaspoons tomato purée
3 egg whites
300ml (½pt) double cream
salt and pepper
15g (½oz) butter

Dressing
2 egg yolks
salt
freshly ground black pepper
1 large bunch chives
juice of ½ lemon
300ml (½pt) *arachide* oil
1 carton soured cream

Skin the sole fillets and drain the prawns *very* well on absorbent paper.

Rinse the green peppercorns under running cold water for 2–3 minutes. Drain well. Peel the carrot and cut into sticks about the size of the beans. Steam the carrot sticks and beans over boiling water until very tender. Rinse under running cold water and drain on absorbent paper.

Set the oven to 175°C/350°F, gas mark 4. Pound the sole fillets and prawns together in a food processor. Season with salt. Place in a large bowl set in a roasting tin of ice. Beat well and gradually add first the egg whites and then the cream making sure that the mixture remains fairly firm. Beat in the tomato purée and pepper. Taste.

Lightly butter a loaf tin or terrine and spoon in a quarter of the pink fish mixture. Spread it flat with a spatula. Arrange 4 parallel lines of green beans down the length of the tin. Cover with a second quarter of the fish mixture. Spread flat. Arrange 4 parallel lines of carrot sticks immediately above the beans. Cover with a third quarter of the fish mixture. Spread flat. Arrange 4 parallel lines of

green peppercorns immediately above the carrots. Cover with the remaining fish mixture and smooth over with a spatula. Cover with a piece of damp greaseproof paper.

Stand the terrine in a roasting tin of near boiling water. Bake for 35–45 minutes. It should feel firm to the touch. Remove from the oven, leave to cool and refrigerate overnight.

Dressing
Put the egg yolks into a liquidiser, add the salt and pepper and whizz until slightly thickened. Add the chives and gradually add half the oil – the sauce should become fairly thick. Add the lemon juice and then add the remaining oil. Add the soured cream and whizz briefly. Taste and add more salt and pepper if necessary. It should be pale green.

Do not worry if the sauce curdles: the soured cream will bring it back together.

To serve
Invert a plate or wooden board over the terrine and turn the whole thing over. Give a gentle shake and remove the tin. Cut into even slices. Pour enough of the chive sauce to just cover the base of a side plate. Cover with 2 slices of fish terrine and garnish with a small sprig of watercress.

Note: If you do not have a food processor the fish should be pushed through a sieve before adding the egg whites (quite a task!).

Julienne of vegetables (serves 4)

340g (12oz) carrots
340g (12oz) courgettes
340g (12oz) leeks
ground ginger
fresh thyme
salt, pepper and butter

Peel the carrots, cut the ends off the courgettes and, using the white part only of the leeks, cut all the vegetables into 'julienne' strips the size of a matchstick.

Wash the vegetables well and steam them separately over boiling water. Season the carrots with salt, pepper and ground ginger: the courgettes with salt, pepper and fresh thyme and the leeks with salt and pepper.

Cook them until just tender and refresh under running cold water until completely cold. Drain well on absorbent paper.

Arrange the vegetables in three neat rows on a large dish. Dot with butter, sprinkle with salt and freshly ground black pepper, cover with clingwrap and refrigerate overnight.

Reheat in the microwave for 8 minutes and serve immediately.

Note: Food reheated in the microwave cools down more quickly than conventionally reheated food and must therefore be served immediately. They can of course be kept warm for a while in the oven but this means removing the clingwrap and covering the vegetables with expensive tin foil. Do not forget that nothing metallic should be put into the microwave oven. Particularly not dishes with a metallic decoration such as gold leaf.

Fresh fruit salad with mango and passion fruit sauce (serves 4)

2 bananas
2 kiwi fruit
2 red plums
110g (4oz) seedless green grapes
1 peach
1 lime
fresh mint

For the sauce
2 passion fruit
1 ripe mango
2 tablespoons water

Put the fruit, unprepared, into the refrigerator for a few hours to chill.

Make the mango sauce. Skin and stone the mango (somehow!). Whizz the flesh with the passion fruit pulp and water, in a food processor. Strain and chill. (If using a liquidiser the passion fruit should be strained before liquidising.)

Prepare the fruit. Skin and slice the bananas into small wedges. Peel the kiwis and slice. Cut the plums in half, remove the stones and slice. Take the grapes off the stalks (if seedless grapes are not available, halve and pip the grapes). Peel the peach, cut it in half, remove the stone and slice.

Spoon the sauce onto 4 pudding plates so that the base is evenly and completely covered. Arrange the fruit attractively on each plate, squeeze with fresh lime juice and decorate with sprigs of fresh mint. Cover with clingwrap until ready to serve.

Index of recipes

Aïllade, 62
Almonds, see Salad, trout; Tuiles aux amandes
Anchoïade de Croze, 79
Apfelstrudel with short pastry, 70
Apple
   charlotte, Dutch, 41
   compôte, 116
   pie, rustic, 121
   snowballs, 34
   strudel, 70
Apricot compôte, 116
Arbroath smokie mousse (and smoked salmon), 12
Aubergines, stuffed, 107

Baked fruit, 116
Barbecued steak or lamb chops, marinade for, 125
Beef teriyaki, 12
Beefsteak Dijonnaise, 89
Bird's nest salad, 134
Blackberry
   and blackcurrant fool, 121
   cheesecake (Betty's), 93
Blackcurrant
   and blackberry fool, 121
   bombe, 102
   and raspberry sauce, 50
   and wine jelly, 37
Brawn, 107
Bread
   healthy, 35
   Sophie McEwen's, 111
Bread and butter pickles, 84
Brioches, smoked haddock, 92
Brussels sprouts (pain de choux Bruxelles), 40
Butter sauce, 50

Cakes
   chocolate (uncooked) and orange, 31
   Christmas, 102
   gilt gingerbread, 134
   hazelnut torte, 67
   honey, 134
   Sachertorte, 70
   See also Caprice Camelot; Coffee meringue gâteau
Caprice Camelot, 98
Carbonnade, curload, 120
Carrots Vichy (with spinach ring), 35
Casseroles
   hare (sweet and sour), 62
   steak, kidney and mushroom, 45
Celebration salad, 27
Chaka, see under Sauces
Champagne sorbet, 143
Cheesecake, Betty's blackberry, 93
Chicken, with lemon sauce, 81
Chicken breasts, stuffed, in summer sauce, 48
Chinese seafood rolls, 97
Chocolate
   filling (for Coffee meringue gâteau), 75
   and orange cake, 31
   pudding (cold), 17
   roulade, 102
Christmas cake, 102
Cockatrice, 133
Coffee meringue gâteau with chocolate filling, 75
Coleslaw, green and red, 92
Collops of lamb with sweet onion purée, 147
Conserve, grape fudge, 84
Consommé madrilène suprême, 11
Cookies, for blackcurrant and wine jelly, 37
Coulibiac, mushroom, with herb sauce, 67
Crab and smoked salmon pancakes, 89
Crayfish, freshwater, 143
Cream
   orange flower, 134
   royale (with clear soup), 79
   tomato, 80
Crème Chantilly, 98
Croquettes
   egg, 128
   potato and celeriac, 62
Crown Diana, 50
Cucumber mousse, 80
Curload carbonnade, 120
Curry of turbot, 67

Damson
   gin (or vodka), 85
   summer pudding, 139
Dutch apple charlotte, 41

Egg
   and bacon pie, Miss Lamont's, 92
   croquettes, 128
Eggs with sherry and orange, 67

Faggots, 22
Fish terrine with chive and lemon dressing, 148
Flan, onion and soured cream, 74
Fool, blackcurrant and blackberry, 121
Freshwater crayfish, 143
Fruit compôtes, 116
Fruit salad, with mango and passion fruit sauce, 149

Game
   pâté, 128
   pie, 54
   puddings, 55
   See also Grouse; Hare; Partridge; Pheasant; Prune and rice stuffing; Rabbit; Venison

Ginger, *see* Medallions of pork; Wild rabbit
Gingerbread, gilt, 134
Glazed shallots, 62
Gnocchi, potato, 116
Gooseberry ice cream, 121
Grape fudge conserve, 84
Green and red coleslaw, 92
Grouse, *see* Game pie; Game puddings

Hamburgers, 125
Hare, *see* Game pie
Hazelnut torte, 67
Healthy bread, 35
Herb
    mayonnaise, green, 27
    sauce, 67
    sorbet, 12
Holkham vegetable pie, 17
Honey
    cake, 134
    ice cream, 50

Ice cream
    gooseberry, 121
    honey, 51
Icing, orange, 31

Jagdwecken, 70
Jelly
    blackcurrant and wine, 37
    fresh basil, 84
Jerusalem artichoke relish, 84
Juice, tomato, 120
Julienne of vegetables, 149

Kastanienberg mit Schlagrahm, 70
Kedgeree, 111
Kiwi fruit, *see* Strawberries and kiwi fruit

Lamb
    barbecued chops, marinade for, 125
    collops of, with sweet onion purée, 147
    crumble, 129
    in a green paste, 22
    shoulder of, stuffed, 49
    See also Prune and rice stuffing
Leeks, *see* Aushak
Lemon chicken, 81
Lettuce soup, chilled, 142
Lime syllabub, 45

Mango, *see under* Sauces
Marinades
    for barbecued steak or lamb chops, 125
    for Beef teriyaki, 12
    for Saddle of venison, 62
Medallions of port with orange and ginger, 98
Melon and peach salad, 135
Meringue
    for Crown Diana, 50
    gâteau, coffee (with chocolate filling), 75
    See also Ritz biscuit torte
Milk shake, 31
Miss Lamont's egg-and-bacon pie, 92

Mousse
    Arbroath smokie (and smoked salmon), 12
    cucumber, 80
Mushroom coulibiac (with herb sauce), 67
Mushrooms, roulette of, 137
Mussel soup, 17

Nut loaf, savoury, 75

Oatmeal pancakes (with shrimps), 138
Old-fashioned stuffed shoulder of lamb, 49
Onion
    purée, sweet (with Collops of lamb), 147
    and soured cream flan (with wholewheat pastry), 74
Orange
    icing, 31
    See also Eggs; Medallions of pork
Orange flower cream

Pain de choux Bruxelles, 40
Pancakes
    oatmeal (with shrimps), 138
    smoked salmon and crab, 89
Parigino, 49
    Partridge, *see* Game pie; Game puddings
Passion fruit
    sorbet, 81
    See also Fruit salad; Sauces, mango and passion fruit
Pasticada Korculanska, 115
Pasties, venison, 92
Pastry
    for Game pie, 54
    for Salmon en croûte, 97
    short, for Apfelstrudel, 70
    wholewheat, for Onion and soured cream flan, 74
Pâté
    game, 128
    smoked salmon, 101
Peach and melon salad, 135
Pear compôte, 116
Pheasant
    pudding, 55
    under a toasted top, 35
    See also Game pie
Pickled pork, 137
Pickles, bread and butter, 84
Pies
    egg-and-bacon (Miss Lamont's), 92
    game, 54
    Holkham vegetable, 17
    pork, 55
    sausage puffs, 45
Pineapple sorbet, 17
Pizza, 107
Pizza people, 31
Pork
    medallions of, with orange and ginger, 98
    in milk, 22
    pickled, 137
    pie, 55
Port and elderberry sauce, 62
Pot roast, 37

Potato
    and celeriac croquettes, 62
    gnocchi, 116
    quiche, 125
Prune
    compôte, 116
    and rice stuffing (for roast game or lamb), 61
Puddings (savoury)
    pheasant, 55
    steak and kidney, 56
    See also Game puddings
Puddings (sweet)
    chocolate (cold), 17
    summer (damson), 139
Pumpkin soup, 74

Queema, see under Sauces
Quiche, potato, 125

Rabbit (wild), in mustard and green ginger, 61
Raspberry sorbet, 102
Redcurrant sorbet, 102
Relish, Jerusalem artichoke, 84
Rice and prune stuffing (for roast game or lamb), 61
Ritz biscuit torte, 89
Roulade, chocolate, 102
Roulette of mushrooms, 137
Royale, cream (with clear soup), 79
Rustic apple pie, 121

Sachertorte, 70
Saddle of venison with port and elderberry sauce, 62
Salads
    Bird's nest, 134
    Celebration, 27
    melon and peach, 135
    spinach and sesame, 121
    trout, and almonds, 142
Salmon
    boiled, 115
    en croute, 97
    See also Smoked salmon
Sauces
    blackcurrant and raspberry, 50
    butter, 50
    chaka, 134
    herb, 67
    lemon, 81
    mango and passion fruit, 149
    mayonnaise, green, 27, 142
    port and elderberry, 62
    queema, 134
    soubise, 139
    summer, 48
    sweet and sour, 62
    velouté, 35, 133
Sausage puff pie, 45
Savoury nut loaf, 74
Sea trout, boiled, 115
Seafood rolls, Chinese, 97
Shallots, glazed, 62
Short pastry (with Apfelstrudel), 70
Shortbread, wholemeal, 121

Shrimps in oatmeal pancakes, 138
Sloe gin, *see* Damson gin
Smoked haddock brioches, 92
Smoked salmon
    and Arbroath smokie mousse, 12
    and crab filling for pancakes, 89
    pâté, 101
Sophie McEwen's bread, 111
Sorbets
    champagne, 143
    fresh herb, 12
    passion fruit, 81
    pineapple, 17
    raspberry, 102
    redcurrant, 102
Soubise sauce, 139
Soups
    clear, 79
    consommé madrilène suprême, 11
    lettuce (chilled), 142
    mussel, 17
    pumpkin, 74
    royale, 79
Spinach ring with carrots Vichy, 35
Spinach and sesame salad, 121
Steak
    and kidney pudding, 56
    kidney and mushroom casserole, 45
    marinade for barbecued, 125
    See also Beefsteak Dijonnaise
Strawberries
    in fondant, 143
    and kiwi fruit, rendezvous of, 13
Stuffed aubergines, 107
Stuffed chicken breasts in summer sauce, 48
Stuffing, prune and rice (for roast game or lamb), 61
Summer
    pudding (damson), 139
    sauce, 48
Sweet and sour casserole of hare, 62
Sweetbreads soubise, 139
Syllabub, lime, 45

Terrine, fish, with chive and lemon dressing, 148
Tomato
    cream, 80
    juice, 120
Trout salad with almonds, 142
Tuiles aux amandes, 143
Turbot, curry of, 67
Turkey, roast, 101

Vegetables, julienne of, 149
Velouté sauce, 35, 133
Venison
    pasties, 92
    saddle of, with port and elderberry sauce, 62
    See also Game pie

Wholemeal shortbread, 121
Wholewheat pastry, 74
Wild rabbit in mustard and green ginger, 61